EXTINCTION
A-Z

ERICH HOYT

✦Environment Reference Series ✦

ENSLOW PUBLISHERS, INC.

Bloy St. & Ramsey Ave.   P.O. Box 38
Box 777   Aldershot
Hillside, N.J. 07205   Hants GU12 6BP
U.S.A.   U.K.

> *To Mose and his cousins and to their generation whose great task, because of the extinction crisis, will be restoring the earth.*

Library of Congress Cataloging-in-Publication Data

Hoyt, Erich.
    Extinction A-Z / Erich Hoyt.
        p.   cm. — (Environment reference series)
    Includes bibliographical references.
    Summary: Presents an alphabetically arranged reference guide to terms and issues relating to plant and animal extinction, and lists laws, government agencies, and public interest organizations that deal with biological extinction.

ISBN 0-89490-325-X

    1. Extinction (Biology)—Dictionaries, Juvenile. 2. Endangered species—Dictionaries, Juvenile. 3. Plants—Extinction—Dictionaries, Juvenile. 4. Man—Influence on nature—Dictionaries, Juvenile. 5. Pollution—Environmental aspects—Dictionaries, Juvenile. [1. Extinction (Biology)—Dictionaries. 2. Rare animals—Dictionaries. 3. Rare plants—Dictionaries.] I. Title. II. Series.
    QH78.H69 1991
    333.95137'03—dc20   90-23701
                                                                       CIP
                                                                        AC
Printed in the United States of America

10 9 8 7 6 5 4 3 2 1

Cover Photo: Ernest Christensen/U.S. Department of the Interior

ACKNOWLEDGEMENTS

I would like to thank Prof. Steven M. Stanley (Johns Hopkins University) for reading the manuscript and offering helpful comments. I am also grateful for interviews and papers provided by Prof. Edward O. Wilson (Harvard University), John J. Fay (U.S. Fish and Wildlife Service), Larry E. Morse (The Nature Conservancy), Linda R. McMahan (Center for Plant Conservation), Calvin R. Sperling (U.S. Department of Agriculture), Peter Raven (Missouri Botanical Garden), J. Trevor Williams (International Board for Plant Genetic Resources), and Vernon H. Heywood (IUCN).

CONTENTS

INTRODUCTION

Extinction means the permanent loss of unique plants and animals—a serious matter facing our world today. The loss can be a species of bird with a certain song, an anti-cancer drug from a plant, or the special, tasty fruit of a tree.

Extinctions of plants and animals have occurred since the start of life on earth. The dinosaurs, for example, became extinct at the end of the Cretaceous period, 65 million years ago. We know about them only from fossils. Such ancient extinctions probably occurred because massive geological events triggered a change in climate. The earth may have turned too hot or too cold for life soon after a volcano erupted, a glacier expanded, or a series of meteorites or comets slammed into the earth.

The French paleontologist Georges Cuvier was the first to point out the fact of extinction. Before 1786, people thought that the end of a species meant that God's creation was imperfect. It was not until Charles Darwin proposed his theory for evolution in 1859 that the story of how life had evolved on earth became clear.

Extinction is a force in evolution. The ancient extinctions paved the way for many new species. Mammals now live where dinosaurs once roamed. In the long-ago past, extinctions happened slowly, over millions of years. And it took a long time for new species to evolve.

Today's extinctions, however, are occurring at a rate a thousand times faster than most of those of past times. Many of the mammals alive today—species of monkeys, wolves, and rhinoceroses—may go extinct in your lifetime. The main cause of their decline is too many people—people polluting air, water, and land; people overhunting; and people cutting down more and more trees for pastures, farms, and a fast dollar.

The tropical rain forests are located in a band around the earth near the equator. They are home to at least 2.2 million species, more than half of the plants and animals in the world. Every year an area of tropical rain forest the size of Kansas is cut or damaged. If the cutting is not stopped, we could lose 1.1 million species in the next few decades. This would mean more than 100 species lost every day, just in the rain forests. And most important: many of these extinctions would be plants and animals that biologists have never even seen or had a chance to study. These plants might have been used to cure diseases or feed the world. We will simply never know the value of what we have lost.

The extinction of a plant or animal reflects on humans as a species—our failure to take care of the earth. It is important that we focus on our responsibility to today's endangered species to save them from extinction.

Extinction A–Z is a dictionarylike survey of many aspects of the extinction problem. This book is designed to show how this key issue affects our world as seen through the interaction of science, technology, and society. This way of looking at the issue will give you a broad base of understanding about extinction and will help you consider what you can do about it.

The book is divided into five sections:

Extinction Terms. A list of about 200 topics surrounding the issue of extinction. The focus is on the modern problem of plant and animal extinctions, but mass extinctions of the past are included as they may shed light on the present. Among the items are:

•Scientific terms defined for their literal meaning as well as their social significance,

•Particular plant or animal species that are endangered and extinct,

•Important events or periods of extinction, and

•Causes, implications, and other aspects of the extinction problem.

This list could be described as the what, why, how, and "what does it all mean" of extinction.

The numbers that follow the main entries refer to specific references in the back of the book where you can go for more information.

Terms Used in the Field. Definitions of the basic terms used by researchers and those working to conserve plants and animals and prevent extinction.

Laws and Agencies. A list of the main laws that deal with the problems of plant and animal extinction—in the United States and around the world—and the government agencies and public interest organizations involved.

For Further Information. The addresses and telephone numbers of government agencies and public interest organizations that can give you added information on plant and animal extinction.

References. The information in this book was gathered from many sources. Some of the most useful of these—for further reading and research—are listed in the back of the book. Each reference is numbered. The numbers after the main entries will direct you to the references that provide more information.

TERMS USED
IN THE FIELD

ADAPTATION. Something about an individual plant or animal of a species that makes it more fit to survive and reproduce compared to other individuals. It can be a special structure, process, or behavior. Natural selection tends to establish adaptations in a population.

ADAPTIVE RADIATION. Evolution from a primitive plant or animal species to many different species, each specialized to a different way of life. Extensive adaptive radiation has occurred after mass extinctions. As new species recolonize the land, they fill the niches left open by extinct species.

AREA-SPECIES CURVE. The graphic plot of the relation between the area of an island and the number of species that live there. The smaller the island, the fewer the species. Biogeographers and ecologists use area-species curves from islands to estimate the number of species that will go extinct when ecosystems are split up or reduced in size, such as by the cutting of the tropical rain forest. In general, reducing an area to a tenth of its original size drives at least half the species extinct. But if the reduced area is smaller than half a square mile, many more than half the species will go extinct.

BIOGEOGRAPHY. The study of how plants and animals are spaced. Some areas are "species rich" and others "species poor." Biogeographers try to find out why plants and animals live where they do. The number of species in a region is a dynamic balance between old species going extinct and new species arriving or evolving.

BIOMASS. The total weight of living things in an area. By looking at the biomass of species or groups of animals or plants, one can compare ecosystems and estimate how productive they are.

BIOME. A type of ecological community spread over a large natural area. There are fourteen main biome types on the land, ranging from tropical humid forests to deserts. These types are based on climate—temperature, rainfall, and other factors.

BIOTA. All of the living things found in a given area. This includes plants, animals, fungi, and microorganisms.

CARNIVORE. A living thing that feeds on animal tissue or flesh. Large animal carnivores are prone to extinction. There are few carnivores per square mile. They need large areas to search for food, and human hunters tend to go after them for sport. Carnivores depend on the health of their prey. If prey species decline, carnivores will not have enough to eat and will decline as well. Contrast with **FRUGIVORE** and **HERBIVORE.**

CARRYING CAPACITY (K). The largest number of individuals of one species that can be maintained in a particular area. Every environment can support only so many individuals. The limits include food, nest sites, shelter, disease, and predators. Ecologists refer to the carrying capacity of the environment by using the letter "K."

COMPETITION. The use of the same resources, such as food or space, by two or more species in an ecosystem in which these resources limit population sizes. When one species wins out, the result can be extinction for the other. This is the case often when exotic species are introduced to an island. Without predators, exotic species soon out-number local species.

CONVERGENCE (CONVERGENT EVOLUTION). When two species from different families evolve to have one or more similar traits or structures. Convergent species, though living in different parts of the world, respond in the same way because they live in and must adapt to similar environments. Convergence has occurred many times in the history of life on earth, yet it can still confuse scientists. Cactus found only in the U.S. West, for example, looks like an unrelated African desert plant. Both have thorns and fleshy stems to store water.

DISJUNCT. A species found in widely separated locales, such as across oceans. Some disjunct species are like living fossils, telling stories of continents that used to be joined. A few of the lichen and moss species found on the west coast of Canada also grow on the coast of Japan.

DNA. A complex material found in the cells of living things. It is the substance of genes. When individuals of a species reproduce, DNA carries the genes into the next generation. DNA is short for *deoxyribonucleic acid*.

ECOLOGICAL COMMUNITY. See **ECOSYSTEM.**

ECOLOGY. The study of the interaction of plants and animals—mainly of plant and animal communities—within their environment. In nonscientific use, it can mean the natural world in general.

ECOSYSTEM. A community of plants and animals in a given habitat, all interacting with one another.

ENVIRONMENT. A plant or animal's surroundings, both living and nonliving. This includes the conditions in which a plant or animal lives, defined by temperature, water, light, and so forth.

ETHOLOGY. The study of animal behavior in the natural habitat. Ethologists want to know how a behavior evolved as well as what may be the immediate cause or trigger of the behavior. This productive way of understanding animal behavior came from Konrad Lorenz and Niko Tinbergen.

EVOLUTION. The process of change through which all plant and animal species, descended from the same simple ancestors, have acquired unique features. Evolution occurs not in individuals but in populations. Evolution may also be defined as the process by which the frequency of some genes changes in the gene pool of a species.

The extensive evidence for evolution is the fossil record, the long record of species living, dying, and changing found in the rocks. Why does evolution happen? Charles Darwin proposed the theory of natural selection in 1859. Since then, this theory of the "survival of the fittest" has been used and tested in millions of experiments. It remains today one of the more productive theories in all of science.

EVOLUTIONARY BIOLOGY. The study of biology applying Darwin's theory of natural selection—survival of the fittest. There are many branches of evolutionary biology embracing studies of animals, plants, ecosystems, and even molecules.

FITNESS. The ability of an individual plant or animal, compared to others of its species, to produce offspring that survive to reproduce themselves.

FOOD CHAIN. The links between living things in a community or ecosystem. Looking at the food chain shows how energy passes from one living thing to another, from plant to animal and from dead animal to the decomposers, bacteria, and fungi.

FOOD WEB. All the food chains between species in a community or ecosystem.

FRUGIVORE. A living thing that feeds on fruit. Frugivores often help spread seeds far and wide. Birds that eat the fruits of tropical rain forest trees, for example, scatter seeds as they eat. Other seeds are swallowed and pass intact through the bird after it has travelled some distance. Contrast with **CARNIVORE** and **HERBIVORE.**

GENE. The unit of inheritance in all plants and animals. Genes consist of DNA. See also **DNA.**

GENE FLOW. The movement of genes between populations and sometimes between different species through migration and inter-breeding. Gene flow is one of the driving forces of evolution.

GENE POOL. All of the genes in a population. Each individual plant or animal of a species will share many of these genes, but only twins or clones will have exactly the same set of genes.

GENETIC DIVERSITY. The variety of genes and genotypes within a particular species. A species is said to be genetically diverse when the number of genes in the population is large. As a rough working number, 500 individuals of a species are thought to be needed for a species to survive. At less than 500 members, the gene pool may be so restricted that the species is doomed. Only by maintaining genetic diversity in a species can wildlife and plant managers effectively fight extinction.

GENETIC DRIFT. A change in the genes of a population or a species from generation to generation due to chance. Genetic drift can push endangered species closer to extinction when populations are reduced to less than a few hundred individuals.

GENOTYPE. The genetic make-up of a plant or animal, including all its genes which may or may not be expressed in an individual plant or animal.

GENUS (plural: **GENERA**). A group of related, similar species. The name of the genus is the first of the two-part Latin name given to a species. For example, two endangered species in the same genus are *Canis lupus*, the gray wolf, and *Canis rufus*, the red wolf.

GESTATION PERIOD. The time between conception and birth. Elephants have a long gestation period—twenty-two months—while for most whale species, it is a year or longer. Mammals with a long gestation period, plus a long time devoted to nursing and parental care, can be vulnerable to extinction.

HABITAT. The place where, or the environment in which, a plant or animal lives. A habitat can be the seashore, the deep sea, or the tundra.

HERBIVORE. A living thing that eats plants. Herbivores are less prone to extinction than carnivores because they often live in larger groups. Contrast with **CARNIVORE** and **FRUGIVORE**.

HOME RANGE. The place in which an animal normally lives. A home range is not defended as a territory. It may be shared with other animals or groups of animals. Some species have territories that they defend within much larger home ranges. Larger animals tend to need larger home ranges. To protect an endangered species, wildlife managers must consider home range. See also **TERRITORY.**

NATURAL SELECTION. The action of the environment on individuals of a species. Those individuals better suited than others to the environment are better able to survive and reproduce. In time, over many generations, a species may split into distinct groups that are each adapted to a special environment. If these groups do not mix, new species will soon evolve. The concept of natural selection is Darwin's proposed mechanism for evolution.

NICHE. A specific role in an ecosystem, such as grass-eating. Can be filled by different species in different areas of the world.

PALEOBOTANY. The study of fossil plants.

PALEONTOLOGY. The study of ancient life, including all aspects of extinct plant and animal life, using fossils and other relevant information. Learning about past extinctions may help us understand the effect of those today.

PHENOTYPE. What a plant or animal looks like. The phenotype comes from genes (from the genotype) interacting with the environment. See also **GENOTYPE.**

PHOTOSYNTHESIS. The food-making process in green plants. A chemical molecule called *chlorophyll* takes in sunlight into the cells of a plant's leaves—the "food factories." There, the sunlight is combined with water from the roots and carbon dioxide from the air to make the tissues of the plant. Life on earth depends on photosynthesis.

PHYLOGENY. The evolutionary history of a group of related species. It is sometimes represented as a "family tree" that shows which species may have given rise to others. The story of how a species has evolved on earth is put together from all related living and recently extinct species, plus species from the fossil record.

POPULATION. A group of individual plants or animals of the same species that live in the same place and are close enough to interbreed.

SOCIOBIOLOGY. The study of social behavior and its genetic basis in all animals.

SPECIATION. The splitting of one interbreeding population of a plant or animal species into two. It is a central process of evolution leading to new species.

Speciation happens most often when part of a species becomes geographically separate. From one species of Darwin's finch that arrived many years ago on the Galapagos Islands, there are now fourteen, each evolving on a different island. New species also arise because they are subject to different environmental conditions, such as different soils.

SPECIES. The basic unit of plant and animal classification. A species consists of plants or animals that can interbreed. The same two-part Latin species names are used throughout the world. To a scientist, the species name of a plant or animal is the key to all that has been written about it. Scientists, conservationists, and industry often argue over species status for endangered plants and animals. Calling something a species can protect an animal or plant under wildlife laws.

SUBSPECIES. A subgroup of a species, a little different from the rest of the species. A subspecies usually occupies a separate region, away from the species. A subspecies can be a "species in the making." A subspecies often has a third Latin name, following the usual two-part species name.

SURVIVAL VALUE. The usefulness of a trait or characteristic in helping a species to reproduce. Individuals having such characteristics, according to the mechanism of natural selection, will contribute more offspring to the next generation. This is how evolution occurs.

SYMBIOSIS. Two or more different species living together in a prolonged, close ecological relationship. There are three types of symbiotic relationships: (1) parasitism—when one species lives at another's expense, (2) commensalism—when one species benefits and the other is neither harmed nor helped, (3) mutualism—when both species profit from the association.

TERRITORY. A space defended by an animal or group of animals against other members of the same or other species. Territories can enhance the survival of a species. The fittest animals, best able to defend a territory, get the best habitat. Wildlife managers must determine the boundaries of an animal's territory in order to conserve its habitat. Animals that need large territories are more prone to extinction due to habitat loss.

ZOOLOGY. The study of animals.

LAWS AND AGENCIES

BUREAU OF LAND MANAGEMENT (BLM). The U.S. federal agency in the Department of the Interior that manages almost half of all public lands—over 272 million acres spread over thirteen western states. Most BLM lands are leased for cattle grazing and mining. BLM lands include many dry and desert-type ecosystems containing threatened and endangered species. Some BLM lands are being considered for conservation as wilderness areas.

CANADIAN WILDLIFE SERVICE (CWS). The Canadian federal agency that carries out wildlife research on federal lands, including national parks, and administers laws on migratory birds as well as the CITES treaty.

CITES—CONVENTION ON INTERNATIONAL TRADE IN ENDANGERED SPECIES OF WILD FAUNA AND FLORA. A worldwide treaty that restricts trade in rare, endangered, and protected species of plants and animals. The treaty was drafted in 1973, and more than 100 countries have signed it. CITES (pronounced SIGHT-ease) countries meet regularly to set rules for the import and export of plants and animals for commercial and noncommercial purposes. CITES has helped protect many species from extinction. Trade in endangered species continues, however, especially by non-signing countries and through the "black market." Also, a CITES rule allows any member country to continue trading in a particular banned species that may be of economic importance.

DEPARTMENT OF FISHERIES AND OCEANS (DFO). The Canadian federal agency responsible for the protection and wise use of whales, dolphins, seals, fish, and other living ocean resources.

ENDANGERED SPECIES ACT. A U.S. law passed in 1973 to protect plants and animals in danger of extinction. Species likely to become endangered may be listed as "threatened." According to the act, endangered species may not be "killed, hunted, collected, harassed, harmed, pursued, shot, trapped, wounded, or captured." The protection for the threatened species varies according to need. All U.S. federal agencies must avoid any action that would jeopardize an endangered or threatened species.

INTERNATIONAL WHALING COMMISSION (IWC). An association of countries set up by treaty in 1949 to manage whale populations. At first, it was little more than a club of whaling nations. In 1986 a motion to stop whaling was passed for the first time, though a few countries have refused to honor the ban.

MARINE MAMMAL PROTECTION ACT (MMPA). A U.S. law passed in 1972, often amended, to protect the "taking" of marine mammals—whales, dolphins, and seals—in U.S. waters or by U.S. citizens abroad. Taking is defined as "harassing, hunting, capturing, killing, or attempting to harass, hunt, capture or kill." Some native Indians and Eskimos in Alaska are exempt. "Takes" are sometimes allowed for scientific research and public display in aquariums. Under current rules fishermen who accidentally catch marine mammals in their gear on a regular basis must sign up for an "exemption program" and report all kills. Some must accept an observer on board. If a species is believed to be in trouble, or if certain fishermen are taking too many, however, the fishing can be stopped. The problem is that there are no population estimates for most marine mammal species.

MIGRATORY BIRD TREATY ACT. A U.S. law since 1918, this act was designed to protect most species of migratory birds from hunting, taking, capturing, or killing, except under permit or during hunting seasons. Some species endangered in times of year-round hunting have recovered because of this act.

NATIONAL MARINE FISHERIES SERVICE (NMFS). A U.S. federal agency responsible for the protection and wise use of whales, dolphins, seals, fish, and other living ocean resources. NMFS helps decide whether oceanic species are threatened or endangered and enforces the Endangered Species Act and the Marine Mammal Protection Act.

NATIONAL PARK SYSTEM (NPS). The U.S. national system of areas set aside for natural, recreational, and historic values and administered by the National Park Service. The main designations protecting natural values are national parks, preserves, and monuments, which comprise 90 percent of the 79-million-acre National Park System. Part of the NPS program has always tried to help threatened and endangered plants and animals. But the small size of some of the parks and the extent of visitor use make the future doubtful for some of the larger endangered mammals.

NATIONAL WILDERNESS PRESERVATION SYSTEM (NWPS). The U.S. system of public lands set aside from industrial use. Since the Wilderness Act was passed in 1964, more than 90 million acres have become part of the system, mostly inside National

Parks, National Forests, National Wildlife Refuges, and, more recently, on BLM lands. In the future, these largely unspoiled lands may be important genetic sources for some rare and endangered species of plants and animals.

THE NATURE CONSERVANCY. A private agency that preserves U.S. lands offering the best examples of many plant and animal habitats. It works closely with state and federal government agencies, as well as colleges, universities, and others, to identify natural areas and find funding for them. The focus is on rare and endangered species.

U.S. FISH & WILDLIFE SERVICE (USFWS). The U.S. federal agency responsible for the conservation of migratory birds, certain mammals, sport fishes, and wild plants. USFWS, along with NMFS, helps decide whether a species is threatened or endangered and enforces the Endangered Species Act. USFWS also manages the National Wildlife Refuges, a separate system of purchased lands outside the public land system.

U.S. FOREST SERVICE (USFS). The U.S. federal agency that manages public lands designated National Forests and National Grasslands. The Forest Service is responsible for maintaining the animals and plants on some 175 areas in thirty-nine states totaling 191 million acres. Most of its work revolves around forestry, but there is a program to identify and manage "sensitive" species before they become threatened or endangered.

WORLD BANK. The world's largest development agency. It was founded in 1945 to help raise the standard of living in developing countries by funding big projects. The World Bank lends money to individual governments and offers economic and technical advice to its 144 country members. Use of the World Bank funds for big dams and certain other projects, however, has been criticized because of long-term damage to the environment.

WORLD CONSERVATION MONITORING CENTER (WCMC). A division of IUCN that provides a data service on conservation. Based in England, WCMC maintains computer databases on threatened plants, animals, and protected areas around the world. The databases provide up-to-date information for planning conservation action to anyone who needs it—government agencies, private individuals, industry, and conservation groups.

THE WORLD CONSERVATION UNION (IUCN). An alliance of some 600 conservation groups and government agencies from 120 countries. It was founded in 1948 as an independent, non-profit organization whose mission is to promote sustainable development and to provide leadership in the conservation of nature and natural resources.

WORLD WIDE FUND FOR NATURE (WWF). Known as **WORLD WILDLIFE FUND** in the United States, it is the largest private nature conservation organization. WWF is based in Switzerland, with affiliates in twenty-three countries. Since 1961, WWF has focused on saving plants and animals from extinction and conserving natural areas in 130 countries.

EXTINCTION TERMS

A

ACID RAIN. A kind of air pollution produced by the release of sulphur oxides and nitrogen oxides into the atmosphere. The main sources are electrical generating plants, smelters, industrial boilers, cars, and trucks. Once airborne, the chemicals are carried by prevailing winds, often for hundreds of miles. Combining with water, they are transformed into acids that fall to earth in rain, snow, or even dry particles. In time, lakes become so contaminated that the fish die. On land, the soil is rendered too acidic to farm. In the forests, the trees lose their leaves.

Acid rain ranks among the worst threats to the environment in the northern hemisphere. In parts of central Europe, whole forests are dying. Damage to the West German timber industry has been estimated at $800 million a year. In Sweden, thousands of lakes have become too acidic for fish. The east coast of North America also has been badly hit. Two hundred and fifty lakes in the Adirondacks of upstate New York have no fish. One rainstorm in Wheeling, West Virginia, was measured at a pH of 1.5—an acidic level between vinegar and battery acid.

As acid rain begins to destroy large areas of plant and animal habitat, some extinctions are likely to occur. In the future, species-rich tropical countries in Asia and South America, with their developing industries, may have a problem with acid rain that could lead to many more species going extinct. See also **HABITAT DESTRUCTION.** (2, 5, 11, 17)

AFRICAN WILDLIFE. The large mammals of Africa—the elephant, rhinoceros, giraffe, mountain gorilla, and others—are under extreme pressure. Since 1900, Africa's large mammal wildlife has been reduced by at least 75 percent. Today, the pressures continue to increase. The main factors are habitat loss, poaching for the wildlife trade, overhunting, and the introduction of livestock.

But the real source of the pressure is the African continent's expanding population—the fastest in history. The needs of so many new people have strained the resources—trees for firewood, land for growing crops and keeping animals, and fresh water. In some areas, deforestation, soil erosion, and desertification have ruined the land. These are the main reasons behind the African famines of recent years. With the destruction of ecosystems that humans depend on, the wild ecosystems where the unique African wildlife lives is being destroyed, too.

Overhunting is behind some of the wildlife losses, but poaching as part of the wildlife trade is more widespread. The wildlife trade is carried on not by tribesmen with spears but by wealthy, well-equipped poachers. In the decade of the 1980s, the African elephant population declined from 1.3 million to 625,000—mainly due to ivory poachers. The demand for cheetah skins for coats has made this fast animal the most endangered African cat species. Measures have been taken to stop the ivory and skin trade for these and other animals, but many species continue to decline.

The mountain gorilla, also a victim of poachers, now numbers less than 300. In the Virunga Mountains of Rwanda, Zaire, and Uganda, about a third of the gorillas left are protected in a model biosphere reserve. The reserve protects the gorillas as well as a watershed forest, vital for the humans, livestock, and crops in Rwanda's lowlands. See also **BIOSPHERE RESERVE, IVORY TRADE, OVERPOPULA-TION**, and **TOURISM.** (2, 3, 5, 13)

AMAZON RAIN FOREST. The world's largest tropical rain forest region, drained by the Amazon River and its tributaries covering much of Brazil and parts of Colombia, Peru, Ecuador, and Bolivia. The Amazon has more than a thousand tributaries, seventeen of them longer than a thousand miles. The original size of the Amazon rain forest was two million square miles—thirteen times the size of California.

The Amazon, like most of the world's tropical rain forests, is being carved up by cattlemen, multi-national corporations, and new settlers. Landless farmers from Brazil's temperate southern region and refugees from the crowded cities have been promised "paradise" in the Amazon. Unfortunately, most of the Amazon is unsuitable for intensive farming or grazing. Once cleared, the land may be productive for a few years, then people must move on, clearing more rain forest.

To date, half of the Amazon's rain forests have been destroyed. At the current rate of cutting, most of the rest will be gone in a matter of decades. The loss of most of the Amazon would lead to the extinction of thousands, perhaps millions, of species. See also **TROPICAL RAIN FOREST.** (2, 5, 7, 12, 13, 16, 17)

AMBER. Fossil tree resin that sometimes contains insects. Amber without insects is sometimes used as jewelry. Looking at amber fossils plus the related living insects, entomologists—insect scientists—can piece together the evolutionary history of the insects they study, much as evolutionary biologists do for birds, reptiles, and mammals.

ANGIOSPERMS. The flowering plants that today dominate the earth. An angiosperm is a plant whose seed is carried in a vessel, such as a fruit. The rise of the angiosperms late in the time of the dinosaurs may explain the diversity in tropical forests today. Before that, tropical forests were covered with gymnosperms such as cycads and conifers. The flowers of angiosperms needed pollinators; thus, special birds, insects, and other animals evolved, along with the plants, as specialists to use the seeds and flowers and carry them far and wide. Today, there are some 250,000 species of angiosperms. The gymnosperms, numbering just 700 species, are mostly confined to northern areas not colonized by the angiosperms and their many pollinators. See also **CYCADS** and **GYMNOSPERMS.** (1, 7, 12)

ANTARCTICA. Called the seventh or last continent, this wilderness at the "bottom" of the world is a fragile yet important ecosystem. A unique land mass, 98 percent of which is covered in year-round ice, Antarctica has few plants and land animals notably penguins. The surrounding ocean, however, is one of the richest marine feeding grounds on earth. There are many species of whales, seals, fish, squid, and numerous birds, most of them depending on vast swarms of krill, a small shrimplike creature.

Through much of this century, Antarctic seas have been plundered and whale numbers reduced to less than 10 percent of their original numbers. In recent years, krill and fish have been "overfished" according to many experts. Year-round research bases on Antarctica, established by seventeen countries including the United States, have made garbage a serious problem. The research, ranging from wildlife studies to studies of the ozone layer, is important. Some geological studies have led to proposals to extract oil and minerals—the most serious threat to Antarctica's fragile ecology. However, the economic gain must be weighed against possible damage to the environment. Shipping oil, for example, is difficult through icy, storm-tossed waters. The effect of even a small oil spill there would be greatly magnified.

Oil slicks could creep under the pack ice, where it would be impossible to clean up and would take many years to break down. The phytoplankton that live on the undersurface of the ice would suffer, as would birds, fish, seals, and all life in the Antarctic's food chain.

In 1975, New Zealand proposed that Antarctica be named a "world park." One hundred and fifty conservation groups have joined in support of this idea. The world park idea envisions full protection for Antarctica with special krill sanctuaries, some scientific activity, and establishment of a special Antarctic environmental protection agency. See also **OZONE LAYER.** (5, 9, 11)

ASTEROID IMPACT. See **EXTRATERRESTRIAL CAUSES OF EXTINCTION.**

B

BACKGROUND EXTINCTION. The rate of extinction, often sporadic, in the course of evolution by natural selection. As species evolve, some go extinct and other lines speciate—divide into more species. Mass extinctions are abnormal events with an increased rate of extinction far above the background rate. To measure the extent of a mass extinction, it is necessary to know the background rate. See also **EXTINCTION** and **MASS EXTINCTIONS.**

BEETLES. Insects of the common, diverse order called Coleoptera. There are more species of beetles than anything else on earth. Beetle authority Terry Erwin, working in the Tambopata forest of Peru, collected enough different species of beetles in a few square miles of tropical rain forest to occupy several lifetimes of study. In trying to explain beetle diversity, Erwin has observed that the further beetles go from their origins, the more specialized they become. Thus, canopy "ground beetles" have evolved disklike feet from which thousands of hairs emerge, each ending in a suction cup. If a land beetle has thirty points of contact, a tree-climbing variety may have 10,000. As more and more of the world's rain forest is cut down, many beetle species are going extinct—some before they are even named or studied. See also **CANOPY (OF THE TROPICAL RAIN FOREST).** (5, 7, 16)

BIOGEOGRAPHICAL PROVINCE. A classification for a specific area of the world with similar climate and vegetation. The world is divided into 207 biogeographical provinces which are in eight biogeographical realms. The Nearctic Realm of North America, for example, has twenty-two provinces, from the Eastern Forest to the Californian.

The system of biogeographical provinces helps point to gaps in the protected areas of the world. Fifteen provinces, for example, have no protected areas. Thirty have five or fewer protected areas and less than 400 square miles protected.

To protect samples of the many ecosystems in each province, a closer look is necessary. Costa Rica is only part of the province called Central America, yet there are a wide variety of ecosystems to be protected—from tropical rain forest to dry tropical forest. See also **COSTA RICA** and **PROTECTED AREA.** (5)

BIOGEOGRAPHICAL REALM. A large region of the world with its own biota. There are eight regions separated by water, deserts, mountains, and climate. (1) Nearctic covers most of North America, except southern México. (2) Neotropical is South and Central America. (3) Afrotropical is all of Africa south of the Sahara and Arabian deserts. (4) Palearctic is all Europe and Asia except for (5) the Indomalayan realm—India and southeast Asia south of the Himalayas and other mountains. (6) Australian is Australia. (7) Antarctic is Antarctica, and (8) the Oceanian realm includes the islands of the open Pacific. See also **CONTINENTAL DRIFT.** (5)

BIOLOGICAL DIVERSITY (BIODIVERSITY). The diversity of all life forms. In common use, it refers mainly to different species of plants and animals. Called *biodiversity* for short, biological diversity is best measured at three levels: genetic diversity, species diversity, and ecosystem diversity. To conserve biological diversity, all three levels must be considered.

Biological diversity is the biological wealth or "capital" of the earth. We need the diversity of wild plants to protect the world's food supply and as a source of future medicines and industrial products. We need the diversity of wild animals including insects to pollinate and spread the seeds of most plants. Plants and animals live together in complex arrangements that have evolved over millions of years. If we break these relationships—by degrading ecosystems and driving species extinct—we may not be able to reconstruct them. Then we will have spent our biological wealth.

In scientific, conservation, and government circles in the late 1980s, "biological diversity" or "biodiversity" became a popular catch phrase. Such awareness helped to increase funding for research and conservation projects in tropical rain forests. Most of it has come through the fund-raising efforts of private organizations such as the World Wildlife Fund. In one year, the MacArthur Foundation gave $7.5 million for tropical rain forests. The National Cancer Institute gave $2.5 million to screen tropical plants for anticancer agents that might be useful for new drugs. The U.S. Congress commissioned a special report on biodiversity, saying that the genes from wild plants "have accounted for about 50 percent of [agricultural] productivity increases and for annual contributions of about $1 billion to U.S. agriculture." Congress has worked on a bill to help conserve genetic diversity. See also **ROSY PERIWINKLE, TAXONOMY** and **TROP-ICAL RAIN FOREST.** (2, 5, 7, 12, 16, 17)

BIOSPHERE. Refers to all life. The sphere inhabited by plants and animals, as opposed to the atmosphere.

BIOSPHERE RESERVE. A type of protected area with a special "architecture" in which one or more strictly preserved core areas are surrounded by a buffer zone where research, tourism, and learning about nature can take place. Outside the buffer zone, people can build houses, grow crops, and cut trees.

Biosphere reserves have three goals: first, to conserve biological diversity and samples of ecosystems—the same goal for most protected areas. Second, to have scientists monitor and do research in the core. Third, to let people see how conservation can work in their lives.

With good conservation, the genes from wild plants in the core area may be used to help the farmers outside the buffer zone. Some trees outside the buffer zone can be cut each year, but the goal is to keep the forest going. Tourists may visit the core area and bring money to the area. Scientists will be able to study wild habitats and make sure the plants and animals stay healthy.

The United Nations, through Unesco, started the Man and the Biosphere Program (MAB) in 1974. Since then, some 269 protected areas in seventy countries around the world have become part of the MAB network. Most large tropical protected areas today are managed using the biosphere reserve concept, even if they are not part of the network. The United States has several biosphere reserves, but much more land is protected in parks and wilderness areas. See also **PROTECTED AREA** and **WILDERNESS AREA.** (2, 5, 11, 17)

BIRD EXTINCTIONS. The end of certain species of birds. As a group, birds evolved, possibly from dinosaurs, several hundred million years ago. Like mammals, they expanded to fill many of the niches left open since the dinosaurs went extinct some 65 million years ago.

More than 100 species of birds have gone extinct since the year 1600. About two thirds of these occurred due to human activities—habitat destruction; use of pesticides or poisons; hunting, including, in some cases, predator control; and the introduction of exotic species such as rats, goats, pigs, sheep, and cattle to islands with unique or endemic species. At least one species went extinct due to a cat brought by a lighthouse keeper to a tiny island off New Zealand. The cat killed all the St. Stephen's wrens found only on that island.

Today there are about 8,600 species of birds. At least 200 are on the U.S. Endangered Species List. Hundreds more are threatened. Currently, an estimated two bird species are going extinct every three years. By the year 2000 that may increase to one bird species per year or more.

Birds reveal much about the health of our world. Feeding at or near the top of the food chain, they acquire pesticides, contaminants, and poisons which may be aimed at insects or other "pests." The pesticide DDT, banned in the United States since 1972, is still used in many other countries. Some birds migrate thousands of miles, depending on healthy ecosystems at both ends of their range and along the way. The need for world-wide conservation efforts and effective treaties to protect birds is urgent. See also **DDT**. (5, 8, 13, 14, 18)

BLACK-FOOTED FERRET (*Mustela nigripes*). America's most endangered mammal, a carnivore in the same genus as minks and weasels. Once common on the Great Plains, black-footed ferrets have teetered on the edge of extinction for four decades. They depended on prairie dogs for food and burrows. As farmers and ranchers killed off most of the prairie dogs, mainly through poisons beginning in the 1930s, ferrets declined too. Many thought these ferrets were extinct, but a colony was found near Meeteetse, Wyoming, in 1981. Four years later canine distemper, a viral disease carried by dogs, nearly wiped out this last colony. Researchers captured the survivors. For two years, the breeding program, staged in eastern Wyoming, had no success. Then in June of 1987 two litters were born. By 1990, there were twenty-four black-footed ferrets in captivity, perhaps some day to be returned to the wild. See also **CAPTIVE BREEDING**. (3, 5, 6, 13)

BOTANICAL GARDENS. Living museums for plants. Like zoos, many botanical gardens are taking part in the drive to conserve biological diversity. Botanical gardens can be used as field genebanks for rare or endangered species, especially those that cannot be stored as seed.

Botanical gardens are also helpful in other ways. The Missouri Botanical Garden in St. Louis, for example, displays endangered plants inside a large dome in a tropical rain forest setting. Museum scientists use the garden's research collection to teach students and the public. In an exchange program with Costa Rica, the museum does research and promotes tropical forest conservation.

Many U.S. botanical gardens take part in a rare plant program organized by the Center for Plant Conservation, based in St. Louis. This valuable program works to conserve plants in botanical gardens and in the wild. See also **BIOLOGICAL DIVERSITY.**

C

CALIFORNIA CONDOR. America's largest bird with a wing span of nine feet. A bird of prey, once numerous, the California condor soared along the west coast mountain cliffs searching for dead meat from México to the Northwest. Today, the species hovers on the brink of extinction. Beginning in the 1800s, they were hunted for sport and as a pest, and their eggs were collected. Like other large birds of prey in this century, condors have been poisoned accidentally by DDT and other predator poisons. Although the adults live up to fifty years, they have only one chick every two years. This limits the chance that the species might be able to return to the wild.

Less than thirty birds remain today in two southern California zoos. A captive breeding program has raised chicks from eggs gathered in the wild. To date, only one pair has bred in captivity. Scientists and conservationists are split on keeping the last condors in captivity. Captive breeding may be their only hope now, but if they are ever to return, more of their habitat must be conserved and improved. See also **CAPTIVE BREEDING** and **HABITAT DESTRUCTION.** (5, 13)

CANOPY (OF THE TROPICAL RAIN FOREST). The upper level of the forest where most of the photosynthesis occurs. In the tropical rain forest, the canopy biome is hot, sunlit, and has many species of plants and insects found nowhere else. It is the richest biotic zone in the world. Recent work on beetles and other insects reveals there may be thirty million species of insects, mostly unnamed and never before seen, mostly in the rain forest canopy. As the tropical rain forest is cut down, many of these species of insects, plus some of the plants, are going extinct. See also **TROPICAL RAIN FOREST.**

CAOBA TREE. The threatened caoba tree from Ecuador, *Caryodaphnopsis (Persea) theobromifolia*, is a wild relative of the avocado. It is resistant to blight, a disease found in California avocado groves. Once a common tree in the lowland tropical rain forest, it was cut down for its wood and to make room for farms and ranches. Today, less than twelve trees remain in a tiny protected forest in Ecuador. See also **WILD RELATIVES OF CROPS.**

CAPTIVE BREEDING. Breeding of captive animals, especially rare and endangered species. About 800 mammal species are now being bred in zoos. One hundred and fifty-four of these are endangered species—about half of all mammals thought to be endangered around the world.

Some of the captive breeding successes are the one-horned rhinoceros, Pere David's deer, Przewalski's horse, and several tiger species. Some species have even been returned to the wild: the red wolf to North Carolina, the Arabian oryx to reserves in Jordan and Oman, and the golden lion tamarin to Brazil.

Certain birds have also been captive bred. A big success has been the peregrine falcon. After zoos had tried and failed to breed them, a long-term program by Cornell University biologists worked. Their techniques have been adopted by several other agencies. The falcons have now been returned to the wild in solid numbers.

One zoo curator says that all zoos could handle 330 species for captive breeding on a long-term basis around the world. But 815 mammals will need captive breeding in the next few years to avoid extinction. Zoos tend to focus on animals that are beautiful or popular. Many species are left out of these high-profile programs.

Captive breeding can be a complex, time-consuming labor of love. Each species has unique needs for breeding. Great advances have been made in recent years in technical accomplishment, but scientific knowledge about endangered species is lacking. The techniques of artificial insemination and embryo transfer mean that rare species housed in facilities around the world can be managed as one large population, with much of its genetic diversity kept intact.

Captive breeding is only part of a species conservation program. By itself it does not save a species from extinction. Once bred, a species must be returned to the wild and its populations built up. Then money must be spent on setting aside enough good habitat. See also **EMBRYO TRANSFER** and *EX SITU* **GENETIC CONSERVATION.** (5, 10, 13)

CAPTIVITY. When an animal is kept in a zoo or aquarium or in any quarters outside of its natural habitat. See also **CAPTIVE BREEDING.**

CARIBBEAN MONK SEAL (*Monachus tropicalis*). An extinct tropical seal about eight feet long and 400 pounds. Once abundant throughout the Caribbean, it was the first animal in the New World recorded by Christopher Columbus. Many sailors, hunters, and traders after Columbus saw the seals as food, fur, and oil. By the late 1600s, the monk seal was the source of a big oil industry that continued, along with the fur trade, through the 1700s and 1800s. In several hundred years, this once common seal was wiped out. The last reliable sighting was near Jamaica in 1952. (4, 13)

CAROLINA PARAKEET (*Conuropsis carolinensis*). An extinct green and yellow parrot that once ranged in great numbers across the U.S. east coast as far north as the Great Lakes and upstate New York.

The painter J.J. Audubon wrote that "flocks of these birds cover [fields] so entirely that they present to the eye the same effect as if a brilliantly colored carpet had been thrown over them." They declined rapidly over a period of 100 years, between the late 1700s and the late 1800s. Because the birds ate grain, farmers shot them. Since they nested in trees, their habitat was displaced when the forests were cut down and human settlements moved in. In the 1880s, sixteen Carolina parakeets were delivered to the Cincinnati Zoo, and two of them survived for three decades: "Lady Jane" and "Incas." As the species dwindled in the wild, the curator tried to breed his last pair. The birds seemed fond of each other, yet refused to mate. In late summer of 1917, Lady Jane died. Incas, the last Carolina parakeet, pined through the fall and winter, dying on February 21, 1918. (4, 8, 13)

CATASTROPHIC EXTINCTION (CATASTROPHISM). See MASS EXTINCTIONS.

CHLOROFLUOROCARBONS (CFCs). A group of chemical compounds used in the manufacture of refrigerants, foam insulation, and solvents, among other things. They are also released by aerosols. CFCs are mainly to blame for damage to the ozone layer, such as the ozone "hole" over Antarctica. See also OZONE LAYER.

CLIMATE or CLIMATIC CHANGE. The prolonged cooling or warming of the earth. When the climate change is abrupt or severe, as it is from time to time in the earth's history, it can cause mass extinctions. Some scientists contend that the fossil record points to global climate change as the main cause of all mass extinctions. But what triggered the climate to change?

Some of it might have been induced by continental drift. In the Late Ordovician and Late Devonian periods, the southern continents, then joined, moved over the South Pole and accumulated large glaciers. There is firm evidence of strong glacial episodes or other climate changes at the times of many of the major extinction events, including the Late Cretaceous period when the dinosaurs went extinct.

Other scientists think that the climate change might have come from meteorites or comets. At least they could have been a factor in some of the climate change. The mass extinction of dinosaurs at the end of the Cretaceous period, for example, took place over several million years, starting well before any extraterrestrial impact happened.

Climate change could also cause future mass extinctions. This time the trigger might be global warming, possibly from the greenhouse effect—human-caused climate change. See also **EXTRATERRESTRIAL CAUSES OF EXTINCTION, GREENHOUSE EFFECT, ICE AGE**, and **OVERKILL HYPOTHESIS**. (2, 5, 11, 15)

CLIMAX or **CLIMAX COMMUNITY.** The final stage in an ecosystem, such as in the life of a forest. Newly forming ecosystems go through a gradual series of changes, or successional stages. Each stage, which can last years or even decades, has different species of plants and animals. The death and decay of species in one period leaves nutrients and sets the stage for the next. The climax tends to be a stable community.

After a forest burns down or is cut, the plant and animal community changes. If climax forest remains nearby, some species will be able to move. But if vast areas are destroyed, extinctions may occur. Knowing the stages of the tropical rain forest is crucial to growing new forests. See also **REFORESTATION** and **RESTORATION ECOLOGY.**

COADAPTATION. See **COEVOLVED RELATIONSHIP.**

COEVOLVED RELATIONSHIP. A relationship between species that have influenced each other's evolution. Symbiotic species—plants or animals that have lived together—sometimes evolve specific structures or traits designed for their interaction.

Examples are certain flowering plants such as orchids that evolved with a single species of wasp, bee, beetle, butterfly, moth, bird, or other pollinator. In many cases only one insect or bird can pollinate the flower. The plant offers the animal food called *nectar*. The flower may even imitate the animal's smell or shape—seeming like a mate. Once attracted, the pollinator finds that its back or other body parts are soon covered in pollen. When the pollinator visits other flowers of the same species, some of the pollen is left behind. The pollinator gets a meal, and the plant is able to reproduce by being cross-fertilized.

Tropical rain forests are old ecosystems with a high number of coevolved relationships. Such relationships mean that if either species goes extinct, the other will soon follow. See also **INSECT EXTINC-TIONS** and **TROPICAL RAIN FOREST.** (7, 10, 12, 16)

COMETS. See **EXTRATERRESTRIAL CAUSES OF EXTINCTION.**

CONSERVATION. The saving of genes, species, or ecosystems from loss or extinction. The word refers mainly to species in nature.

To conserve a species in nature, three main things are needed: (1) basic knowledge about the species such as numbers, distribution, social behavior, feeding, habitat requirements, and mode of reproduction; (2) a large enough number of individuals to make sure the gene pool is conserved; and (3) enough natural habitat with food, water, and other requirements to support the population.

Over the past decade, the driving force for conservation, especially in the tropics, has been protecting a sample of each ecosystem. Protected areas that effectively conserve sample ecosystems will save many plant and animal species from extinction. Yet many more and much larger protected areas are needed around the world—especially in tropical forests. A type of protected area called a *biosphere reserve* is an effective way to include local people in the process of conservation.

Another aspect of conservation for some endangered species is captive breeding. This has helped some animals to return to the wild. But in general, keeping an animal in captivity by itself is not conservation. In the artificial conditions of a zoo or aquarium, an animal cannot continue its evolutionary path.

Plants, too, require a protected habitat to continue to evolve. In addition, many conservation programs use seed banks and botanic gardens, keeping seeds and plant samples, to reintroduce and enhance wild populations. See also **BIOLOGICAL DIVERSITY,** *EX SITU* **GENETIC CONSERVATION,** *IN SITU* **GENETIC CONSERVA-TION, and PROTECTED AREA.** (2, 5, 11, 13, 17, 18, 19, 20, 21, 22, 23, 24, 25, 26, 27)

CONTINENTAL DRIFT. The gradual drifting apart of the world's continents. Near the end of the Paleozoic Era 200 million years ago, there was only one land mass and an enormous ocean. Over several million years, this land mass split in two around the equator. Slowly, these two then broke up into the continents that we know today.

The evidence that the continents were once joined can be seen in the way South America, for example, seems to fit into Africa. But India was actually part of east Africa. When they separated, India moved north, hitting Asia with such force that it pushed up the largest mountains in the world, the Himalayas.

The movement of the continents has played a role in the evolution and extinction of many plants and animals. As the continents separated, ocean currents changed, causing marine species to go extinct. The separate continents also divided populations of land species so that in time they became new species. When some land masses rejoined, such as India to Asia, some land species went extinct. In general, the more divided the land masses became, the more chances for new evolutionary pathways and the more species diversity. See also **LAND BRIDGE.** (14, 15)

COOLING. See **CLIMATE** or **CLIMATIC CHANGE.**

CORAL REEFS. Found in shallow tropical seas, coral reefs are the richest and most complex marine ecosystem. They are formed mainly from the fused shells or skeletons of living sea animals. Reefs can extend for hundreds of miles parallel to shore. The living reef provides homes for a bright array of odd-shaped tropical fish. The reef also acts as a buffer zone between the beach and the open sea, protecting the land from erosion.

Many coral reefs have been destroyed. "Reef mining" is part of several developing countries' economies. The limestone shells are used for building material, ground into polish, or burned to make pure lime. But coral reefs also attract tourists. If managed well, coral reefs—as well as some of the unique species that live there—will have a future. (2, 5, 13, 17)

COSTA RICA. This small country in Central America has a model system of protected areas. About 10 percent of the country is conserved in a diverse sample of its ecosystems. But Costa Rica also has a high rate of deforestation. By the year 2000, it will become the first country in Latin America to lose all of its tropical rain forests that are *not* protected in parks.

Costa Rica has a large foreign debt. When the unprotected forest is all cut, there will be pressure to exploit the forest remaining in parks. What options will the country have? Costa Rica is a significant country in terms of the overall fate of the world's tropical rain forests: What happens there today could be, for better or worse, the future for the rest of tropical Latin America.

International conservation groups and other agencies are working with Costa Ricans to develop an economy based on the principles of sustainable development. See also **PROTECTED AREA.** (2, 7)

CRETACEOUS PERIOD. The geological period in the earth's history from 65 to 144 million years ago. During this period, long before humans evolved, dinosaurs roamed the earth. At the end of the period, however, the dinosaurs and many marine animals—about half of all species then alive—died in a mass extinction. See also **DINO-SAURS** and **MASS EXTINCTIONS.**

CYCADS. Called "living fossils," cycads are among the oldest plant families in the tropical rain forest. They are gymnosperms—plants with naked seeds. Cycads survived the dinosaur age and the rise of flowering plants, the angiosperms, which now cover the earth. Like angiosperms, cycads take advantage of pollinators—this may be one secret to their survival. With about 100 species, cycads range in size from a few feet to up to fifty feet tall. These evergreens prefer the shady understory of the tropical rain forest. See also **GYMNO-SPERMS.**

D

DAMS. Massive structures built to block rivers and generate electric power. In recent years, dams have helped developing countries like Brazil to provide jobs and power for new industries. But the cost to the environment can be high.

Dams can destroy plant and animal life through the flooding of land as well as the pollution of river water from contact with flooded land. Also, the process of making electricity means that the water is heated then returned to the river. Many marine plants and fish die as a result.

The world's largest dam, built in the Paraná River along the border of Brazil and Paraguay, flooded many thousands of acres of tropical forest, destroying habitat and killing plants and animals. Many local populations were reduced, and some species may have gone extinct. (11)

DDT. A pesticide used to control insects. DDT stands for *d*ichloro*d*iphenyl*t*richloroethane. Developed in the 1940s, DDT was mainly used in agricultural sprays. It has been banned for use in the United States since 1972, yet it lingers in the environment. U.S. chemical companies still make DDT for export to other countries.

DDT was banned because it breaks down very slowly in the environment. It can last for years in lethal or near-lethal amounts, stored in the tissues of plants and animals. DDT causes reproductive failure in birds and fish, especially those feeding at the top of the food chain. DDT nearly wiped out peregrine falcons and other birds of prey. In recent years, with captive breeding and release and no more DDT, peregrines have returned to the U.S. east coast. Eagles, too, are on the increase. But birds that migrate to Latin America where DDT is still used are declining.

DDT's effects on wildlife are far reaching. Even Antarctic penguins, thousands of miles from the nearest direct source, have been found with DDT in their fat. See also **PEREGRINE FALCON.** (5, 11, 13, 17)

DEBT-FOR-NATURE SWAPS. See **DEBT IN THE DEVELOPING WORLD.**

DEBT IN THE DEVELOPING WORLD. Money which developing countries such as Brazil and México owe banks and governments in developed countries, mainly the United States and Japan, totaling more than $1 trillion. The huge national debt of countries in the developing world is part of the reason tropical plants and animals are threatened. To pay the interest on their debt, these countries must raise quick cash by selling crops, trees, land, and other natural resources. Many economists recognize that the debt can never be repaid. Yet these countries continue to become poorer and their biological resources are ruined for what uses that country and the world might make of them. Part of the solution may well have to be forgiveness of the debt, but the banks are reluctant to set a precedent.

A partial solution in recent years has been debt-for-nature swaps in which conservation groups have purchased the debt in exchange for conservation agreements. In 1987, Bolivia agreed to create a 3.7-million-acre rain forest reserve in exchange for forgiveness of $650,000 of its external debt. Conservation International purchased the debt at a discounted price of $100,000 from the banks. This is a small part of Bolivia's $5.8 billion external debt, but the area to be protected is substantial. Since then, Costa Rica, Ecuador, and other tropical countries have announced "debt-for-nature swaps." See also **TROPICAL RAIN FOREST.** (2, 11)

DEEP-SEA LIFE. A diverse group of animals that live at great depths in the ocean. In 1977 a new deep-sea ecosystem was found—at a depth too deep for photosynthesis yet teeming with life. These strange life forms were new species of worms, clams, and blind white crabs. They were found clustered around hot vents in the ocean floor where they depend on bacteria.

Deep-sea life, around the vents and far out to sea, is threatened. Many countries dump sewage sludge and toxic industrial waste far from their shores in the deep sea. See also **MARINE POLLUTION.**

DEFORESTATION. Cutting trees, usually over a large forested region. It also implies the practice of cutting trees without replanting them.

From earliest times, the wealth and progress of the world's civilizations have been built on using forests. They were cut for firewood, to build houses, and to make room for crops and livestock. Today, multinational logging companies buy land or obtain leases to do their cutting in many parts of the world.

In the temperate north, the large scale cutting of the forest began in Europe 1,000 years ago. Today, much of this primitive, original forest is gone, even in North America. Some of the remaining primitive forests in Canada and the United States are known to hold rare and endangered species, such as the spotted owl. Many scientists believe that these old forests should be saved for research and as gene pools for future forests. Government programs conserve pieces of the primitive forest but some feel these sections are too small to support endangered species.

Since the early 1900s, overall forest cover in the temperate zone has stayed about the same. Some of the forest has regenerated naturally and reforestation, or replanting, in this zone has improved. In recent years, though, acid rain and air pollution have begun to slowly kill many northern trees—a new form of deforestation.

In the tropics, about half of all rain forests have been eliminated—the most dramatic change to the earth's biosphere. Over the next thirty years, most of the rest of the tropical forest may go and with it half of the earth's species. Compared to temperate forests, tropical forests are more complex and tend to have poorer soils. They take hundreds of years to grow back. In some areas they may never grow again.

When forests are cut down, the carbon dioxide levels in the atmosphere increase. This may add to global warming from the greenhouse effect, which some scientists believe has started or will start soon. But a temperature rise could also come from the loss of evaporation of moisture after too many trees are cut down.

Most of the environmental tragedies in tropical countries, such as famines, floods, droughts, and fires, can be traced to the loss of forests. See also **FOREST ECOSYSTEMS, GREENHOUSE EFFECT, REFORESTATION**, and **TROPICAL RAIN FOREST.** (2, 5, 7, 11, 12, 16, 17)

DESERT ECOSYSTEM. A place where ten inches of rain or less falls every year. Cold deserts, or tundra, caused by extreme cold, are at the polar ice caps. Warm deserts, often with sandy soil, form one fifth of the earth's surface. These large deserts lie north and south of the equator, around the Tropic of Cancer and Tropic of Capricorn.

Desert ecosystems are true deserts, created by nature, as opposed to those created by desertification through human misuse of the land.

True deserts have some rainfall and a limited number of plant and animal species that have evolved to live there. Desert plants and animals are specially adapted to collect, conserve, and build their lives around the limited moisture that they find.

Many desert species are threatened or endangered. In the dry U.S. southwest, these include the ocelot and many species of cactus and wild beans. Desert plants are valued for their ability to survive in a dry, hot world. In the future, if the greenhouse effect makes the earth hotter and drier, desert areas may expand. To adapt crops to these changing conditions, scientists may need the genes from wild desert plants. See also **DESERTIFICATION, GREENHOUSE EFFECT**, and **WILD RELATIVES OF CROPS.**

DESERTIFICATION. Turning wild lands, mainly drier and desert ecosystems, into barren, lifeless wastes, through human misuse of the land. When dry or semi-dry regions are overgrazed or used for growing crops, they can lose their fertility. The soil is then exposed to wind and water erosion. In time no plants can grow here. With no plants there are no animals.

These human-made "deserts," are sometimes called false deserts. True deserts are the fragile desert ecosystems that do support plant and animal life. Desertification mainly occurs in true deserts and along their margins. But even forests, once stripped of their trees and if allowed to erode, can become desertified.

Desertification is a severe world problem. Every year 50 million acres of new false deserts are created. The problem is most severe in Africa where two of every five acres of non-desert left are at risk of desertification.

With desertification, the world is also losing such valuable desert species as the addax, a desert antelope of Africa that can go without water for many months at a time. The addax could be used as a food source in a part of the world where meat is hard to come by. But, gone from most of its former range, it is now endangered. A reserve in the country of Niger has been set up, and scientists are now studying the addax to learn how it survives in the desert. See also **DESERT ECOSYSTEM.** (2, 5, 11, 17)

DINOSAURS. Name generally used for a group of large extinct vertebrates represented by two different animal orders: Ornithiscia and Saurischia. Both orders became extinct about 65 million years ago near the end of the Cretaceous period.

Dinosaurs thrived for more than a hundred million years. They were the dominant animals on land. Mass extinctions result when animals cannot adjust to sudden and severe changes in their environment. Yet the precise cause of the dinosaurs' mass extinction, which occurred as many marine organisms also went extinct, has long been the subject of debate. Many scientists hold that it was a meteorite or comet that crashed into the earth. See also **EXTRATERRESTRIAL CAUSES OF EXTINCTION** and **MASS EXTINCTIONS.** (14, 15)

DODO BIRD (*Raphus cucullatus*). An extinct bird that once lived on the island of Mauritius in the Indian Ocean. These bulky gray birds were up to more than three feet long and fifty pounds. They had small wings—too small to fly. On an island with no predators, they had no need to fly. They were abundant but confined to the island. Soon after Portuguese sailors arrived in the early 1500s, ship crews began eating the easy-to-catch birds. They declined sharply in the 1600s and went extinct about 1690. The word "dodo" survives in the English language to mean a stupid person. (4, 8, 13)

DUSKY SEASIDE SPARROW (*Ammospiza nigrescens maritimus*). A canary-size bird species, never very widespread, that went extinct in 1987. Earlier in this century, thousands of dusky seaside sparrows flew through the marshes of Florida. Their habitat was drained, cut with roads, and sprayed with pesticides. Over two decades, the Florida Audubon Society tried to save the bird but failed. A rescue mission, launched in 1979, found only five males. The last male, old and half-blind, lived in a pen at Walt Disney World's Discovery Island in Florida. There he died on June 16, 1987. (13)

E

EARTH DAY. A day celebrated in the spring of 1970 when conservationists gathered in many places all over the United States in support of protecting the earth. This demonstration occurred at a time when some people were beginning to see the threat of overpopulation, pollution, and loss of plant and animal species. This growing worldwide concern helped set the stage for the environmental movement of today. In 1990, on the twenty-year anniversary, a new "earth day" was celebrated. This time, millions more participated.

ECOLOGICAL RESTORATION. See **RESTORATION ECOLOGY.**

ECONOMIC BOTANY. The study of plants used by humans for food, shelter, clothing, medicine, and other products. Most of them—corn, wheat, rice, apples—are cultivated, but some are wild: certain oil palms, Brazil nuts, and old growth timber. These and other plants are crucial to the economies of the world. Today, countries are starting to see that biological diversity is a source of economic wealth. See also **ECONOMIC PLANTS.**

ECONOMIC PLANTS. Plants used by humans for food, shelter, clothing, medicine, and other products. Today, humans depend on less than one percent of living plant species for existence. Many others are potentially useful but untried—and some will go extinct before we discover their full value.

Half of all the world's food, for instance, is provided by three species—rice, wheat, and corn—and 90 percent of our food comes from twenty species. Yet there are about 75,000 edible plants.

Most medicines come from plants. Quinine, which comes from the bark of the cinchona tree, is a remedy for malaria. Curare, made from the bark and stems of a vine found in the Amazon, is used to relax muscles during surgery. The rosy periwinkle of Madagascar now helps to cure leukemia in children and Hodgkin's disease. An estimated one in ten plant species has some anti-cancer activity, yet few have been studied.

Many other products also come from plants. Certain palm trees yield oil for detergents, plastics, and fuel. The leaves of another palm tree provide the materials for car wax and shoe polish. Cotton provides raw material for clothing. Oils for perfume and soap come from trees, many of them tropical.

The value of wild plants toward producing crops, medicines, and industrial products is billions of dollars per year. Yet potential economic plants will be going extinct if the cutting of the tropical rain forest continues. To insure our future food supply and the use of industrial and medicinal plants, it is important to conserve wild plants and the wild relatives of crops and other economic plants around the world. See also **BIOLOGICAL DIVERSITY, ECONOMIC BOTANY**, and **WILD RELATIVES OF CROPS.** (7, 12)

ECOSYSTEM DECAY. See **MINIMUM CRITICAL SIZE OF ECOSYSTEMS PROJECT.**

EMBRYO TRANSFER. A technique, commonly used in domestic animals, in which an egg is removed from a female animal, fertilized out of the body, and transferred to another female. Embryos can be frozen and transported around the world.

Zoos are now using embryo transfer with endangered animals in captive breeding programs, as well as with females in the wild. In some cases they have even split the embryo of the endangered animals and transplanted the two halves to two surrogate mothers. See also **CAPTIVE BREEDING.**

ENDANGERED SPECIES. A plant or animal species in danger of extinction in all or a main portion of its range. "Endangered" is a legal status under the U.S. Endangered Species Act. The term is also used in state legislation and in the Red Data Books. To control world trade in endangered species, most countries have signed the CITES agreement. See also **ENDANGERED SPECIES LIST** and **RED DATA BOOKS.** (3, 5, 6, 7, 9, 12, 13, 18, 20, 21, 22, 23, 24, 25)

ENDANGERED SPECIES LIST. List of plant and animal species in danger of extinction in all or a main portion of their ranges. "Endangered" is a legal status under the U.S. Endangered Species Act.

The list was started when the act was passed in 1973. New species are added all the time. A few have been taken off, as species become extinct or recover, or new research reveals that the species was not endangered.

When a species is "listed," it may not be "killed, hunted, collected, harassed, harmed, pursued, shot, trapped, wounded, or captured." It also means that U.S. government agencies must not harm the species in the course of their activities. The Forest Service, for instance, cannot let trees be cleared if that might destroy an endangered bird or mammal habitat. But, if there is no alternative and the action is economically sound, then the agency can proceed with development. See also **CITES** and **ENDANGERED SPECIES ACT** (both under **LAWS AND AGENCIES**). (3, 5, 6, 13)

ENDEMIC SPECIES. A plant or animal species that is confined to one region of the world, often an island or a refugium. Compared to species that live in many parts of the world or on continents, endemics are more vulnerable to extinction. The threat is not just due to a small, confined habitat. Many endemics, such as those on islands and in refugia, evolved in the absence of mammal predators. They are defenseless when exotic predators are introduced.

On Hawaii, for example, two thirds of the endemic bird fauna has gone extinct this century. And most of the endemic plants on the Galapagos Islands, the Balearic Islands, Ascension Island, and Mauritius are threatened with extinction. See also **EXOTICS, HAWAIIAN ISLANDS**, and **REFUGIUM**.

EVOLUTIONARY RATES. The pace of evolution is uneven. The fossil record shows that at times in the past evolution occurred rapidly. More often, evolution has been slow. A common trend has been for evolution to occur rapidly early in the history of a group.

***EX SITU* GENETIC CONSERVATION.** Conserving plants or animals "off site," out of their natural habitat, as opposed to in the natural habitat, *in situ*. Plants are conserved *ex situ* either as seeds in genebanks, or as tissue cultures or plants mainly in botanical gardens. Animals are conserved *ex situ* in zoos, aquariums, or zoological parks.

Species kept in genebanks or in zoos are "frozen." Without pressure to adapt to changing natural conditions and to compete with other species, they stop evolving. But when life in the wild becomes tough, *ex situ* genetic conservation may be the best way. In time, the population may be rebuilt and the wild habitat restored. The captive breeding of the California condor and the black-footed ferret are examples of such a last-ditch effort. But for the effort to have the best chance of success, sufficient genetic diversity must be conserved. The rough guide is a minimum of 500 individuals, but it depends on the species. For mammals in zoos, 275 may be enough. Certain plant species have been built back up from only a few dozen plants. The future for most animals reduced to only a few breeding pairs is less certain.

Ex situ (in captivity) and *in situ* (in the wild) genetic conservation are sometimes argued as an either/or case. Zoos and botanical gardens push the case for captive breeding. Other conservationists, on the other hand, will press for setting aside habitat as the only route, no matter the expense. Today, more and more people see that both strategies must be used. See also **CAPTIVE BREEDING, GENEBANK**, and *IN SITU* **GENETIC CONSERVATION.** (5, 13)

EXOTICS. Species introduced to an area. The arrival of a new species may upset the balance of an ecosystem. Exotic species have left their predators behind. In the fight for limited food or space, exotics can drive native or endemic species to extinction. Rare and endangered animals and plants are the first to go.

In Hawaii, for example, exotics have out-competed native plants and animals, leading to many extinctions. Before humans brought domestic and other animals and plants and cut down the rain forest, Hawaii was a much more diverse place. About two-thirds of Hawaii's bird species are now extinct.

Other exotic organisms spread or cause diseases. In the United States, the gypsy moth, chestnut blight, and Dutch elm disease have lessened America's native diversity. See also **ENDEMIC SPECIES** and **HAWAIIAN ISLANDS.**

EXTINCTION. The end of a species. Some scientists refer to the end of a species in part of its range as local extinction. Also, a distinction is sometimes drawn between a species that may end only because it has evolved into something else (pseudoextinction) and extinction that is the end of a lineage of organisms (terminal extinction). Terminal extinction is the usual meaning of the word extinction.

Ninety-nine percent of all life that has ever lived on earth is now extinct. Indeed, without these extinctions over several billion years of the earth's history, evolution as we know it could not have happened.

Extinction is an important force in evolution. The ancient extinctions paved the way for many new species, such as the mammals replacing the dinosaurs. Historically, extinction is a natural process that takes place when a species is unable to adapt to a changing environment or to compete with better-adapted species.

The causes of a single species going extinct often cannot be deduced from the fossil record. But for mass extinctions—crises on a global scale—the causes are a matter of theory supported by, in some cases, good evidence. Only for recent extinctions (those since 1600) can we determine with some certainty the factors leading to extinction.

Three-quarters of all extinctions since 1600 have occurred on islands. This is because islands tend to have a superb variety of odd species that evolved in isolation and are only found in that one place. When humans arrive, bringing exotic species and guns and destroying habitat, these endemic island species have nowhere to go.

Today's extinctions occur at a rate at least a thousand times as those in the past. They are mostly human-caused. Hunting has forced a few animals to extinction. But bigger impacts come from too many people polluting air, water, and land, and cutting down too many trees—especially in the tropical rain forest. Yet even if we stop altering the environment, it will take millions of years after the current mass extinction for life to recover. See also **BACKGROUND EXTINC-TION** and **MASS EXTINCTIONS.** (2, 4, 5, 8, 11, 13, 14, 15)

EXTINCTION PULSES. As viewed in the fossil record, minor peaks in the number of extinctions. Thus a mass extinction may be made up of a few pulses spread over a period of time, often hundreds of thousands or millions of years.

EXTRACTIVE PRESERVE. See **GENETIC RESERVE.**

EXTRATERRESTRIAL CAUSES OF EXTINCTION. The idea that certain mass extinctions on earth may have been caused by such things as the arrival of meteorites or comets, or changes in the sun's output of radiation. The main evidence comes from a thin layer of clay with the element iridium, found in the fossil record near the end of the Cretaceous period at sites around the world. Iridium is rare in the earth's crust but common in meterorites. In 1980, U.S. physicist Luis Alvarez first proposed his theory: 65 million years ago, when a mountain-size meteor hit the earth, the dust kicked into the air blocked the sun and stopped photosynthesis. Plants withered and animals, including the dinosaurs, starved.

Some scientists question the theory. They say that iridium could come from volcanoes and that volcanic eruptions caused the mass extinction. Others believe that the meterorites brought the iridium but that it did not cause the mass extinctions. They think that the mass extinction of the dinosaurs was underway before the impact occurred. They point out that dinosaur extinction appears to have happened over a long period of time.

Since 1980, there have been more theories and evidence for the "impact scenario." One theory is that a star passing close to the sun could have sent millions of comets flying, a few of them hitting the earth over a period of hundreds of thousands of years.

Further study of the fossil record has revealed the presence of two amino acids rare on earth. They are only found in the layers at the end of the Cretaceous period when the mass extinction occurred. In the same layers are quartz grains with planes of distortion thought to come from shock. This type of quartz is found near impact craters. One such crater of just the right age lies under fields in Manson, Iowa. It is twenty-two miles wide.

Much more work needs to be done to verify extraterrestrial causes of extinction. See also **MASS EXTINCTIONS, DINOSAURS**, and **PERIODIC EXTINCTIONS, THEORY OF.** (14, 15)

F

FAUNAL INTERCHANGE. See LAND BRIDGE.

FIELD GENEBANK. A place for conserving plant genes as whole plants or trees growing in a cultivated plot, such as in botanical gardens. A field genebank takes up more space than a seed bank, yet cannot cover the full range of genetic diversity of a species or maintain it as it lived in the wild. These collections are also prone to the spread of disease. Yet for some species that cannot be conserved as seeds or tissue cultures, a field genebank is the only way. Some of the crop species found in field genebanks, both cultivated varieties and wild relatives, are cocoa, rubber, and bananas. See also **SEED BANKS, TISSUE CULTURE,** and *EX SITU* **GENETIC CONSERVATION.** (5, 11)

FIELD STUDIES. Research done in nature with wild plants or animals. In the 1830s Charles Darwin made a five-year trip mainly around South America to see the natural world. It led to his theory of evolution by natural selection. It also led to generations of scientists who saw field studies as crucial to an understanding of biology.

Much of that changed with the molecular biology revolution of the 1950s and 1960s. Although some biologists continued to do fieldwork, many others felt there was little left to learn in the field. Molecular biology has revealed much about the workings of genes and

DNA, but the real-world "laboratory" still calls. Studies in ecology, conservation biology, and taxonomy—all of which are based on good fieldwork—are crucial to the survival of species and for setting up protected areas.

Recently, a growing number of biologists have returned to field studies. They are using new equipment and techniques such as radio monitoring and DNA analysis to learn about genetic diversity. They have fresh theories to test as they take another look at species as diverse as whales and ants and acacia trees in their natural habitat.

A pressing need is a biological inventory. Today, as many as 90 percent of the species on earth remain unnamed and unstudied. Most are in the tropical rain forest and half may go extinct in the next few decades. Many of the new field biologists hope that as government and the public become more aware of the extinction crisis, more funding for field study projects will become available. See also **BIOLOGICAL DIVERSITY** and **TAXONOMY**.

FOREST ECOSYSTEMS. Land covered in trees, ranging from open woodland to closed forest types. There are three main types of forest: cold forests with mainly conifer trees, temperate forests with mixed deciduous trees, and tropical forests. Before the start of agriculture 10,000 years ago, forests covered some 15.3 billion acres—60 percent of the earth's land. Today, with half of the tropical and a fifth of the temperate forests gone, there are 10.4 billion acres left—only 40 percent of the land.

Trees form the base of many natural systems. They provide food for animals. They protect soils from erosion. They anchor river and stream banks. Trees hold moisture in their leaves and offer it up to the clouds as rain for the whole planet. They support ecosystems with the greatest diversity of life on earth—the canopy of the tropical rain forest. Trees also play a vital role in the global cycling of carbon. The more trees we have, the better the earth will be able to handle global warming from increased carbon dioxide: the greenhouse effect. See also **DEFORESTATION, REFORESTATION**, and **TROPICAL RAIN FOREST.**

FOSSIL (OR GEOLOGICAL) RECORD. The story of life on earth as told through fossils. The earth is about 4.6 billion years old, but there are few fossils before the Cambrian period which began about 570 million years ago. Most species lived and died without a trace. The fossil record is only a small sample of all the species that ever lived—mostly the history of "hard parts" such as bones, shells, and teeth. Soft parts rarely fossilize because they decay so fast. The Burgess Shale of Canada, some 550 million years old, is an exception.

The fossil record tells us about past extinctions. It gives us clues as to how the evolution of life has occurred. It may also hint at what the future holds. See also **EXTINCTION.**

FUR TRADE. See **WILDLIFE TRADE.**

G

GENEBANK. A place for conserving the genes of plants, especially crops and related wild plants, out of their natural habitat. Three types of genebanks are used: seed banks (for seeds), field genebanks (for plants and trees), and tissue culture (for parts of plants). See also *EX SITU* **GENETIC CONSERVATION, FIELD GENEBANK, SEED BANKS,** and **TISSUE CULTURE.** (5, 11)

GENETIC ENGINEERING. Techniques to make genetic changes in plants or animals by manipulating DNA. Also called *bioengineering* or *gene splicing,* it is part of the larger field called *biotechnology.*

 Genetic engineering has many possible future uses. In the near future, plant breeders will continue to create new crops through lengthy breeding, bringing in new genes from many cultivated varieties and wild relatives of the crop. But genetic engineering should soon speed up the process through direct transfer of genes. Distantly related wild plants will be able to be used as sources of genes. This means that genetic engineers of the future will be looking for genetic diversity—a much wider pool of material. Almost any plant species, if conserved, could be useful in the future. See also **WILD RELATIVES OF CROPS.** (2, 12)

GENETIC EROSION. The loss of genetic diversity in a plant or animal species. It occurs when individuals in a population or even

64

whole populations are lost. The cause can be habitat destruction, hunting, poisoning, or the introduction of exotic species.

When the habitat is reduced, genetic erosion often occurs at the edge of a species' range. The result is that outlying populations are lost and with them special traits such as the ability to live in an extreme climate or resist a certain disease.

Genetic erosion is very hard to measure species by species, but the loss of wild forests, grasslands, and other natural habitats around the world means that it is happening almost everywhere.

Severe genetic erosion can hurt an endangered species' chances for survival. The variety of genes in the overall gene pool is what allows a species to continue adapting to conditions in the wild. See also **GENETIC DIVERSITY** (under **TERMS USED IN THE FIELD**). (5, 11)

GENETIC RESERVE. A type of protected area set aside to conserve the gene pool of one or more species. Seeds and cuttings are made available for research and plant breeding. Recently, scientists in India set up their first "gene sanctuary" for wild relatives of citrus trees, which may be useful for crop breeding some day. They are also planning other genetic reserves for wild banana, sugar cane, rice, and mango. See also *IN SITU* **GENETIC CONSERVATION** and **PRO-TECTED AREA.**

GEOLOGICAL TIME. The time scale for major changes in the earth as seen in the fossil record. Many of these changes occur over millions of years. See also **FOSSIL RECORD.**

GIANT PANDA (*Ailuropoda melanoleuca*). An endangered mammal, distantly related to bears, once common in mountainous central China. One of the more popular animals because of its large size and attractive black and white markings, the giant panda needs a large home range to support the different species of bamboo it feeds on.

The giant panda has been declining mainly due to hunting and destruction of its habitat for thousands of years. In the 1970s, many starved to death following a massive die-off of bamboo. By the early 1980s, less than 1,000 were left in the wild.

Tens of millions of dollars have been spent on panda research and habitat, yet the species continues to decline. The chief threat today is poachers. Despite stiff laws in China, the animals are killed for their skins, worth thousands of dollars each.

About 100 pandas are in captivity in China and in zoos around the world. Keeping them captive is debated among conservationists because only about 30 to date have been born in zoos—an even lower rate than in the wild. See also **POACHING.** (3, 5, 13)

GLACIATION. See **ICE AGE.**

GLOBAL RESOURCE INFORMATION DATABASE (GRID). Computer data showing detailed world maps with soil, vegetation cover, land use, weather, and many other aspects of the world environmental picture. The information is sorted and synthesized from satellite pictures and detailed surveys. The United Nations Environment Program (UNEP) has put together this database to help scientists, conservationists, and government planners from around the world to manage their resources.

GRAY WHALE, PACIFIC. (*Eschrichtius robustus*). A species of baleen whale that grows up to forty-six feet long and thirty-five tons. Found today only in the North Pacific, gray whales were once common in the North Atlantic and North Pacific, but were eliminated in the North Atlantic around 1750 in part due to whalers. Their bones are still found on the beaches of the U.S. east coast.

Gray whales in the North Pacific were whaled in the nineteenth century mainly off the California coast and in the lagoons of Baja California, México. Their blubber was made into oil and oil products. By the 1920s they were so scarce that one report called the species extinct. The few gray whales left were among the first to be protected by the International Whaling Commission in 1946. Today, the Pacific gray whale is believed to be at or near the carrying capacity of the environment, at 19,000–22,000 animals. It is a conservation success story. (3, 5, 6, 9)

GREAT AUK (*Alca impennis*). An extinct black and white bird once common along the rocky shores of the North Atlantic from the Gulf of St. Lawrence, Canada, in the west, to Norway in the east, and as far south as France. Up to thirty inches long, this appealing bird was the original penguin. The penguins of the Antarctic were named after it.

The great auk's feathers were prized for decoration and their eggs by collectors and for food. Impossible to catch in the water, great auks were helpless once on land where they crawled out every year to lay eggs on bare rocks and feed their young. The early Norse visits to America may have been inspired by the migration patterns of great auks. Certainly the Norsemen used the birds for food. By the late eighteenth century few were left. The species was last seen alive in 1844 on the island of Eldey off Iceland. On June 3 of that year, sailors killed the last known breeding pair and sold the skins to a collector. (4, 8, 13)

GREAT PERMIAN EXTINCTION. The mass extinction of the late Permian period, about 250 million years ago. The most severe extinction of all time, it is though to have eliminated 75 to 90 percent of all then-living marine species. See also **MARINE MASS EXTINCTION.**

GREENHOUSE EFFECT. The warming of the earth's atmosphere due to excess carbon dioxide. Like glass in a greenhouse, carbon dioxide in the atmosphere traps most of the heat radiated from the earth when light from the sun strikes its surface. Without carbon dioxide, the earth would be too cold for life. But too much carbon dioxide could make things too hot.

In recent decades, the amount of carbon dioxide in the atmosphere has risen by a quarter. It has come mainly from the burning of coal, oil, and wood in factories and houses, and from cutting down forests. Scientists predict that the amount of carbon dioxide will double in the next sixty years. That could cause a three degree centigrade rise in world temperature.

The effects from such a rise would be dramatic. It would be warmer on earth than it has been for 100,000 years. And the rate of increase would be at least ten times faster than the last Ice Age. Aftereffects could include melting of the polar ice caps with a rise in sea level. This would put many coastal cities under water and destroy coastal ecosystems. Global warming would also lengthen the dry season for ecosystems inland. Changes could occur so fast that animals and plants would have trouble adapting. There could be many more extinctions than after the last Ice Age.

One plan to help species is to conserve long "natural corridors," unblocked by roads or fences, connecting protected areas. By moving along the corridors, some species could change habitats, such as from an area that is increasingly dry to one similar to the one in which the animal had evolved. These ideas might help a few animals, but the outlook for many species is poor. Many animals and plants would have to be moved.

Some scientists believe that global warming has begun; others think that it may start soon. No one knows how the earth will respond. Maybe the ocean can take up more carbon dioxide than it does now. Maybe humans can find ways to temper the effect. The nations of the world are starting to take steps to stop global warming but the costs to industry are high. Tough measures must be taken. Even then, it may only slow down the adverse effects. See also **DEFORESTATION** and **DESERT ECOSYSTEM.** (2, 11)

GYMNOSPERMS. The non-flowering plants, such as pine or other conifers, whose seeds do not develop in an ovary or fruit. See also **ANGIOSPERMS.**

H

HABITAT DESTRUCTION. Destroying the land or water where plant or animal species live. It is the main cause of plant and animal extinctions today. There are many forms of habitat destruction: clearing land for houses, farms, or cattle ranches; oil spills; marine pollution; and dams. Other causes include acid rain and the greenhouse effect. The worst destruction—and the most damaging to biological diversity—occurs in the tropical rain forest. See also **DAMS, DEFORESTATION, OIL SPILLS,** and **TROPICAL RAIN FOREST.**

HAMBURGER CONNECTION. The link between the U.S. appetite for hamburgers and the destruction of about half of the tropical rain forest cut in Central America. In the past twenty-five years, fast food chains have bought beef cheaply from cattle ranchers in tropical countries, especially in southern México. Buying beef there made U.S. hamburgers about five cents cheaper. To make this business more profitable, the ranchers cut down the forest to make more cattle pastures. But this practice can harm the environment. After seven to ten years, cattle destroy the thin, fragile rain forest soils. Then more forest must be cut for new pastures.

Cutting the tropical rain forest can only provide cheaper beef and higher profits for a few more years. Then the forest will be lost for its other values, mainly as a source of biological diversity.

After the press exposed the "hamburger connection," some fast food outlets stopped buying the cheaper beef. They did not want to be responsible for helping to destroy the tropical rain forest. See also **BIOLOGICAL DIVERSITY** and **TROPICAL RAIN FOREST.** (12)

"HANDS-OFF" POLICY. Managing a plant or animal species by leaving it alone. Some conservationists think the best way to help a wild species, even if it is endangered, is to let it live on its own once the habitat is protected and threats such as poaching are removed. The "hands-off" policy allows the animal or plant to stay wild; it remains in its environment, subject to evolutionary pressures. But it may also then be subject to extinction. After much argument over the California condor, for instance, the choice was made to retrieve the eggs from the wild to be hatched in captivity and eventually to rescue all the remaining free animals. The species was too close to the edge. See also **CALIFORNIA CONDOR.**

HAWAIIAN ISLANDS. Because of its mid-Pacific tropical locale, Hawaii has many endemic plants and animals living on a string of volcanic islands. But houses, tourist resorts, pineapple plantations, military bases, and the introduction of exotic species have damaged most of the islands.

In the diminishing tropical rain forests of Hawaii, for example, about sixty land bird species have gone extinct this century. Only twenty-eight known bird species are left and just nine have healthy populations today. These bird extinctions have had other effects. The extinction of several species of honeycreepers drove a Hawaiian flowering tree to extinction in 1912. Hau Kuahiwi (*Hibiscadelphus wilderianus*), the name of this beautiful tree, needed the honeycreepers for pollination. As the honeycreepers one by one became rare or went extinct, the tree declined and disappeared. See also **HONEYCREEPERS.** (4, 5, 8, 13)

HONEYCREEPERS. A number of diverse species of honeycreepers (family Drepanididae), found in Hawaii, which seem to have evolved from a single finchlike bird species. This ancestor colonized the islands one by one and gave rise to at least twenty-two species. In the absence of such birds as parrots, woodpeckers, or hummingbirds, the new species of honeycreepers have filled those niches. Through a process called adaptive radiation, some honeycreepers have evolved beaks fitted, like woodpeckers or hummingbirds, to certain insects or to nectar; others are parrotlike, feeding on flowers and fruit. Today, 40 percent of the honeycreeper species are extinct and 40 percent are endangered. Most of the extinctions occurred in the late 1800s after a century or more of decline. The extinctions came from cattle grazing, introduced species that brought diseases, and the cutting of the forest. See also **HAWAIIAN ISLANDS.**

I

ICE AGE. The interval of glaciation in the northern hemisphere that began in mid-Pliocene time about 3 million years ago. It continued through the entire Pleistocene epoch and ended as the last glaciers receded 11,000 years ago. During the main part of the Pleistocene, there were twenty episodes of glaciers spreading then receding. Many of them may have caused extinctions of plants and animals. Some scientists believe we are still in the Ice Age and that a new glacier will descend from the north in a few tens of thousands of years. See also **CLIMATE** or **CLIMATIC CHANGE.** (14, 15)

IMPACT SCENARIO. See **EXTRATERRESTRIAL CAUSES OF EXTINCTION.**

IN SITU **GENETIC CONSERVATION.** Conserving plants or animals "on site," that is, in their natural habitat, in enough numbers to make sure the gene pool is conserved. Species conserved this way continue to evolve with other species of their ecosystem.

In recent years there has been much talk about the need to conserve wild "genetic resources." But wild genetic conservation is costly. Detailed scientific studies with lengthy field surveys are needed to determine the requirements of each species. What each species needs then must be weighed against using the land for its oil, timber, mineral, and other resources. These are the economic and political costs of

conservation. See also **CONSERVATION** and **GENETIC RESERVE.**
(5, 11, 13)

IN VITRO CONSERVATION. See **TISSUE CULTURE.**

INSECT EXTINCTIONS. The end of certain species of insects. As a group, insect extinctions are harder to chart than birds or mammals. Insects arose about 400 to 500 million years ago, but it was not until about 300 million years ago that they resembled those alive today. Scientists study the outlines of insect evolution and extinction through fossils—many of them made out of amber.

The reasons for insect extinctions in the past century include habitat destruction and the use of pesticides. As with birds, mammals, and plants, the greatest diversity of insects is in the tropical rain forest. This is also where the greatest number of extinctions must be occurring—as about half the tropical rain forests of the world have been cleared in recent decades. New work in the canopy of the tropical rain forest reveals there may be more than 30 million species of insects in the world. Yet only about 750,000 have names.

Although less appealing than birds or mammals, insects have an important role. Ants and termites, for example, do most of the turning of the earth's soil—far more than all the human farmers. Ants are the dominant animal in the tropical rain forest—about one third of the entire animals biomass (the combined weight of all mammals, birds, fish, and insects). By one estimate there are 200,000 ants for every human on earth.

If ants have the numbers, beetles have the diversity. Beetles are found all over the world but nowhere are there as many species as in the tropical rain forest. There may be millions of beetle species, more than all the other plant and animal species combined, and most of them are yet to be named.

Insects share with birds and some mammals the crucial role of pollinators. The rise of these pollinators around the time of the dinosaurs led to the modern era of flowering plants, the angiosperms. Their wide diversity today can be seen in the tropical rain forest in plant groups such as the orchids. Certain bees have coevolved with orchids and other flowering plants. If the species of bee goes extinct, the orchid species will soon follow. See also **ANGIOSPERMS** and **COEVOLVED RELATIONSHIP.** (7, 13, 16)

IRIDIUM. An element rare in the earth's crust but common in meteorites. Its presence around certain fossils has been used to explain why dinosaurs went extinct. See also **EXTRATERRESTRIAL CAUSES OF EXTINCTION.**

IVORY TRADE. The business of selling the tusks of elephants. Though other animal bones and teeth are sometimes used, African elephants are the main source of the world's ivory. A small amount of "legal" ivory comes from elephants that die naturally or are culled. ("Culls" are sick, injured, and often old individuals that are killed as part of a wildlife management program.) But most of the ivory has come from poachers. The poachers sell it to smugglers or dealers who manage to get around the CITES convention, set up to control the world wildlife trade. CITES covers only raw ivory. So traders get the carving started in Africa, then ship it to Hong Kong and Japan for detailed work. From there, ivory statues, jewelry, and trinkets have been shipped around the world. Until recently, most finished ivory ended up in the U.S. and Japan. In 1990 a new amendment to CITES banned all ivory trade. At the same time, the United States has banned all ivory imports.

Before poaching increased in the 1980s, elephants were already losing numbers because of habitat destruction. In the decade of the 1980s, the African elephant population declined from 1.3 million to 625,000. Poachers kill whole herds of elephants. But the mature animals—those with the most ivory—have been the hardest hit. Elephants do not start to mate until their thirties. With a gestation period of twenty-two months, this means it could take years for the species to recover, even if the killing stops. If the slaughter continues at the present rate, the elephant will be near extinction by the year 2000. Scientists and conservationists are working hard now before numbers get much lower. See also **OVERHUNTING, POACHING**, and **WILDLIFE TRADE.** (2, 5, 13)

K–L

KEYSTONE SPECIES. A plant or animal species that is critically linked to many other species in its ecosystem. Some scientists think that if a keystone species goes extinct, many other species will go with it and the entire ecosystem will collapse.

On the west coast from California to Alaska, for instance, the fur traders drove sea otters to near extinction. It also changed the near-shore ecosystem of the sea otters. Sea otters had always eaten large amounts of shellfish including sea urchins. Without sea otters, the sea urchins ate their way through the surrounding kelp or seaweed forests. Once the kelp was gone, fish, including commercial species such as herring, declined, as well as predators of fish such as dolphins, harbor seals, and eagles.

In recent years sea otters have returned through re-introduction programs. Slowly, their ecosystems have begun to return to health.

Other keystone species may be the gopher tortoise, the elephant, and the rhinoceros. In tropical rain forests, the keystone species concept may not apply. These forests are so complex. Yet in some areas, scientists have pinpointed bats and figs as key species.

The keystone concept is not shared by all. Some scientists think that we don't know enough about species (most of which have never been studied) and the relationships between all the species in an ecosystem to favor one species over another.

LA BREA PITS or **RANCHO LA BREA TAR PITS.** Tar pits of Los Angeles, California, where there are masses of the bones of birds and mammals from the Pleistocene epoch. Many of these animals went extinct about 11,000 years ago. The pits tell the story of herbivores, perhaps in search of water, who got caught in the tar. Then they became bait for carnivores, such as the extinct sabertooth tiger, who came in great numbers for the feast and died in the trap. But the La Brea pits did not cause any extinctions. For causes, see **OVERKILL HYPOTHESIS** and **CLIMATE** or **CLIMATIC CHANGE.** (14, 15)

LAND BRIDGE. A piece of land joining two large land masses such as continents. Land bridges arise due to the elevation of land or the lowering of sea level.

Land bridges have played a crucial role in the extinction of species in North and South America. About two to three million years ago a land bridge formed between the continents at Panama. After tens of millions of years apart, North and South America had no mammals in common. As they were joined, wolves and large cats from the north swept across South America. A few northern species went extinct, but mostly they killed off or displaced the south's carnivores. Other mammals moved north, such as anteaters, spider monkeys, opossums, and armadillos, but few pushed further north than México.

This "faunal interchange" between North and South America made both continents richer in mammal species and families at first. But over time the extinctions left both continents with close to the same number as they had at the start. See also **MAMMAL EXTINCTIONS.** (14, 15)

LAND USE. The way a piece of land is or may be used. Who owns the land or controls its use is a key factor in land use decisions. Land use questions often arise in conservation debates. Is the habitat of an endangered species partly farm land, a cattle ranch, or housing subdivision? Is it a wilderness area on public land or a national park? Forested land may be leased to large logging companies. Concessions, even in park or on private land, may be given to mining companies.

Land use patterns vary in different places—from the temperate zone to the tropics, from country to country, from river valleys to mountain tops. They also vary in time—from the feudal estates of the Middle Ages to modern day democracies or dictatorships.

Conservationists and wildlife managers must assess the present land use patterns and the future prospects, region by region and country by country. This is part of setting up good protected areas and saving plant and animal species from extinction. See also **PROTECTED AREA** and **PUBLIC LANDS.**

M

MADAGASCAR. A tropical island, twice the size of Britain, 250 miles east of Africa in the Indian Ocean. It is almost a "mini-continent" in its diversity of climate and terrain, supporting unique species of plants and animals.

Since humans arrived about 1500 years ago, most of the forest has been cut down. The people who live on the island depend on farming. Each year they cut more and more forest to grow crops and graze cattle. Many unique species have gone extinct and others live on the edge.

Madagascar is the only place where lemurs, a major primate group, survive. From at least thirty-five species of lemurs, there are now twenty-two left. Other extinctions include two species of giant tortoises and up to twelve species of large flightless elephant birds, the biggest birds ever.

The island may have 8,500 species of plants, about 6,500 of which are found nowhere else. Some of these, such as the rosy periwinkle, are cures for different types of cancer. Scientists, backed by conservation groups, are in a race against time to study the species left there before they go extinct. See also **ROSY PERIWINKLE.** (3, 5, 12, 13)

MAMMAL EXTINCTIONS. The end of certain species of mammals. As a group, mammals are fairly recent in origin—200 million years old. They kept a low profile during the "Age of Reptiles." After the dinosaurs went extinct about 65 million years ago, the "Age of

Mammals" began. New species of mammals evolved to fill many of the niches left by dinosaurs. Then, about 40 million years ago, a mass extinction of mammals occurred. Many species were lost, but as a group mammals recovered.

More recent extinctions have occurred during the Ice Age that began 3 million years ago. Since the Pleistocene epoch started 1.8 million years ago, some twenty episodes of glaciers spreading and receding have caused extinctions from both cooling and warming. Near the end of the Ice Age, hunting also played a part. Early humans, as well as their ancestors, were mostly hunters. In pursuit of large mammals, they drove extinct some of the large mammal species in Africa, Europe, Asia, and North and South America. Some scientists believe that hunting may have caused half or more of all of these recent large mammal extinctions.

In more recent times, wherever humans have gone—to large islands with unique animals like Madagascar and Mauritius—similar extinctions have occurred.

Today there are about 4,100 species of mammals. An estimated 815 will need to be bred in captivity soon to avoid extinction. But even if all the zoos in the world take part in captive breeding, they can only handle about 330 species on a long-term basis.

Mammals, such as whales and the giant panda, are among the most appealing life forms on earth. They attract millions of dollars to conservation. Because of their size, they need large habitats that cost more to conserve. The smaller or less appealing mammals—everything from the hundreds of rare rodent species that few scientists have studied to the noisy sea lions shot on sight by fishermen—are also worthy of study and conservation efforts. See also **EXTINCTION.** (3, 4, 5, 6, 13, 14, 15)

MANGROVES. Tropical trees that grow in a dense tangle with many prop roots in muddy salt water swamps. They are found along thousands of miles of coastline in tropical South America, Asia, and Africa.

Mangroves have aerial roots that arch from the trunk and help support the trees. Living mostly in sea water, mangroves tolerate salt in their sap. They secrete salt from their leaves and roots. Mangrove roots provide homes for barnacles, sponges, algae, and corals—the basis for a whole community of fish and other marine animals.

Mangroves also reduce coastal erosion, but many countries are cutting their mangrove forests. The tidal zones where they grew are being turned into marinas or are claimed for rice and other farming.

The mangrove forests support coastal marine life in the tropics. As they are cut, the whole ecosystem goes with them. See also **WETLANDS AND AQUATIC ECOSYSTEMS** and **WETLANDS DESTRUCTION.** (5, 11, 12, 13, 17)

MARINE MASS EXTINCTION. The loss of marine life as revealed in the fossil record. The first known mass extinction, about 650 million years ago, killed algae at a time when the first animal life was starting to move into the sea. Later marine crises killed off trilobites (an ancient group of invertebrate animals), large armored fish, and many other diverse groups of marine organisms. But nothing matched the mass extinction of the late Permian period, about 250 million years ago. The most severe extinction of all time, it is thought to have eliminated 75 to 90 percent of all then-living marine species. The causes of these mass extinctions are debated. See also **MASS EXTINCTIONS.** (14, 15)

MARINE POLLUTION. Introducing to the ocean unnatural products (such as PCBs or plastics) or natural substances, but at unnatural levels. More and more in recent years, the ocean has been used as a dump for human and industry waste. The sea can handle some of this waste. But studies show that the ocean may not be able to break down or absorb every kind of material, such as toxic chemicals and radio-active waste.

Most marine pollution comes from the land—farms, city sewage systems, factories, nuclear reactors, and oil refineries. Chemicals or pesticides get into rivers, first killing life there before flowing out to sea. Ocean currents than carry the pollution all over the ocean, even into deep sea trenches.

The sea has become a dangerous cocktail of chemicals and other contaminants. When an animal washes up dead on a beach, it is hard to find the exact cause of death. All animals, including humans, carry levels of contaminants in their body tissues. But which ones, combined with which others at what levels, cause harm or death? Scientists need to do more research.

Marine pollution threatens many species of seals, crustaceans, fish, plankton, and other marine life. Those at the top of the food chain—especially marine mammals—are the first to show the effects of pollution. The chemicals concentrate in their body tissues. Dolphin and porpoise species that feed close to the shores of North America, for example, have high DDT, PCB, and mercury levels. In recent years, belugas or white whales have been dying in high numbers in the St. Lawrence River in the province of Québec. The cause is thought to be the high levels of toxins and contaminants some of which come from cities in the Great Lakes region such as Detroit, Buffalo, Cleveland, Toronto, and Montréal. Belugas are protected from hunting or whaling, yet pollution may yet kill them in the St. Lawrence. See also **OIL SPILLS.** (2, 11, 17)

MASS EXTINCTIONS. The loss of large numbers of species, all over the earth, as revealed in the fossil record. There have been about twelve mass extinctions since the first known mass extinction 650 million years ago. Most have occurred partly on land and partly in the sea. They last for extended periods, sometimes millions of years.

Extensive adaptive radiation has occurred after each of these crises in the history of life. As new species recolonized the land and sea, they filled the niches left open by extinct species.

Scientists disagree on the causes of mass extinctions. Many say that climate change—mainly the flow and retreat of glaciers—has been the most frequent factor. Animals that liked warmth died out when it became too cold, while those used to cold died out after the glaciers left. Some think the climate change came after large volcanoes erupted or when continents drifted over the South Pole. Others favor extraterrestrial theories—that meteorites or comets struck the earth and that dust from the impact blocked the sun, causing a massive die-off. A few scientists think that the meteorites or comets may have fallen at regular intervals, causing most of the mass extinctions we see in the fossil record.

According to some scientists, we are now in a period of mass extinction that is happening faster and may be worse than those that went before. This time, the cause is human, through such things as the burning of fossil fuels, which produces acid rain and may be leading to global warming, and the cutting of the tropical rain forest. Unlike previous mass extinctions, which seem to have involved mostly animals, this time many plants are going, too. See also **CLIMATE** or **CLIMATIC CHANGE, EXTINCTION**, and **EXTRATERRESTRIAL CAUSES OF EXTINCTION.** (2, 4, 5, 7, 8, 11, 12, 13, 14, 15, 16)

MEADOWFOAMS. Several species of rare wild plants (*Limnanthes*) found in the U.S. Northwest. The seeds have been found to have a high quality oil for electronic equipment and drug products. To develop an economic crop, plant breeders need access to all meadowfoam species, but the nine known species are all candidates for the endangered species list. Their habitat has been displaced by farms and ranches. Conservation efforts are underway to protect them in seed banks and genetic reserves.

MINIMUM CRITICAL SIZE OF ECOSYSTEMS PROJECT. A research program with U.S. and Brazilian scientists to find out the best sizes for tropical rain forest reserves. This long-term experiment in the Amazon of Brazil is comparing test plots of 2 1/2 acres, 25 acres, 250 acres, 2,500 acres, and 25,000 acres. The plots are islands of wilderness surrounded by farms, ranches, and clear-cut areas. From time to time the species of plants and animals in each area are counted at the edges and in the deepest part of the forest to determine the number of extinctions.

The researchers have found that deep forest species are lost quickly in reserves of 2 1/2 or 25 acres because of the hot, dry conditions at the edge of the forest that take over the whole area. A plot of 250 acres appears to be the minimum size for a stable reserve. For maximum diversity, there should be a 100-yard-wide forest corridor linking nearby reserves.

As the tropical forest is cleared all around them, the study will continue. The researchers are seeing the long-term effect of "fragmentation" of the forest. The hope is that the Brazilian government—and other countries with rain forests—will listen to the researchers' suggestions. See also **PROTECTED AREA** and **TROPICAL RAIN FOREST.** (5, 16)

N

NATURE RESERVES. See **PROTECTED AREA.**

NORTHERN RIGHT WHALE. A large baleen, or plankton-feeding, whale about thirty-five to fifty feet long and up to fifty tons. With only 300 to 350 left in the North Atlantic and even fewer in the North Pacific, the northern right whale is the whale closest to extinction. It has been nearly extinct since the early 1900s. (There are also fewer than 3,000 southern right whales, mostly off Argentina in the South Atlantic.) The estimated pre-whaling population of all right whales was 50,000.

Beginning in the eleventh century, right whales were killed off the coast of Europe. By the year 1530 they were so scarce that European whalers had to move across the North Atlantic to what is now eastern Canada and the United States to find them. By the late 1700s few were left in the North Atlantic, and the whalers moved to the North Pacific. The right whale was one of the first whales to be killed in great numbers. Whalers prized the right whale, giving it the name "right" because it was slow and often floated when harpooned—the "right" one to kill. It also offered abundant oil and other products. One 50-ton right whale could be made into 80 barrels of oil.

In the early 1980s, a population of right whales was found in the Bay of Fundy on the North American east coast. The good news pushed researchers to work year-round to try to find all the whales, identify them, count them, and monitor their health. No one knows if there are enough right whales left to stage a comeback. (6, 9)

NUCLEAR WINTER. The aftereffects of a nuclear war, which could cause darkness day and night for months on end from clouds of dust, smoke, and other debris in the atmosphere. Such prolonged darkness over large parts of the earth would stop photosynthesis and make it much colder. Many plants and animals would go extinct.

O

OIL SPILLS. The accidental spilling of oil into the ocean. Some 6 million tons of oil find their way into the ocean each year. Most of it enters the sea as run-off from the land, mainly around cities. About one quarter is spilled into the sea by accident, mainly from oil tankers. The cause of most accidents can be traced to human error, but world regulations have been recognized as inadequate. Small oil tanker accidents are common. Each year, many happen that are not publicized. Only large oil spills make headlines.

In March of 1989, the tanker *Exxon Valdez* ran aground on Bligh Reef, Alaska, spilling 10 million gallons of crude oil through Prince William Sound and the Gulf of Alaska. The oil slick spread quickly, but Exxon was slow to help in the clean-up. Yet even with a fast response, clean-up crews can only take care of a small percentage of an oil spill. As the Exxon oil was blown ashore by wind and waves, millions of sea birds, seals, fish, and crustaceans were affected. A number belonged to threatened or endangered species. The oil lowered body temperatures, causing some animals to freeze to death. Others had damaged livers, kidneys, and lungs. A few birds and sea otters were able to be saved. The full impact on animal populations, however, will take years to assess.

Most tanker accidents occur within five miles of land. If the oil washes ashore or covers coral reefs, the damage to marine life may last for decades. In the fragile Antarctic it could last for centuries. A recent oil spill in one area there, small compared to the Exxon spill, may disrupt the food chain for all marine life, from krill to penguins.

The world uses oil to heat homes and to run factories, cars, and other vehicles. We use more and more oil each year. We use so much that demand stays high and regulations tend to be few. Shipping oil by tankers at sea is cheap and convenient, but the costs to the environment can be high. Fishing and tourist industries suffer huge economic losses. Oil spills make the headlines and are a serious problem, yet compared to the dumping at sea of human and industry waste, oil spills are only a small percentage of all marine pollution. See also **MARINE POLLUTION.** (2, 11, 17)

OVERHUNTING. Killing too many animals for meat, sport, or commerce. Overhunting has helped cause a number of extinctions. Stone Age hunters are believed to have killed large mammals such as the mammoth, giant sloth, and cave bear, possibly driving them to extinction. This "overkill hypothesis" is favored by some scientists, while others believe that the climate change from one or more episodes in the last Ice Age played the main role.

Since 1600, overhunting has been the main factor in the extinctions of the Carolina parakeet, the passenger pigeon, the elephant bird, and the moas. In the early history of humans, hunting for meat may have driven a few species extinct, especially if they were rare or endemic species. Controlled hunting such as hunting for dear meat, though, does not usually threaten wildlife populations. But hungry human hunters are not choosey. Endemic species of deer have been driven extinct in southeast Asia, and many other species of mammals and birds have been hunted to very low levels.

Sport and trophy hunting has also played a role in endangering wildlife. In the late nineteenth and early twentieth centuries, rich European and Indian big game hunters spent their time shooting animals and seeing how many they could kill. One Englishman was reputed to have killed 500,000 birds and mammals. The tiger was the trophy of prestige. Two maharajahs alone killed more than 2,000 tigers, and claimed they were sorry they could not have killed more. In many cases, the sought-after animals tended to be fine examples of rare species in their prime, those that should be left alive to maintain the genetic strength of the species. "Safari clubs" still meet in the United States and many countries to compare notes, show off trophies, and make plans for future hunts. Today, their effect on wildlife populations is minimal compared to commercial hunting for the wildlife trade, including poachers.

Overhunting in the wildlife trade continues to be a major cause of endangering wildlife. Elephants are killed for their ivory, cheetahs and jaguars for their skins. See also **IVORY TRADE, POACHING**, and **WILDLIFE TRADE.** (3, 4, 5, 8, 13, 14, 15)

OVERKILL HYPOTHESIS. The proposal that hunting by roving bands of Stone Age humans was the main cause of the large mammal extinctions of Pleistocene. The case is best argued in the Americas where the extinctions occurred close to 11,000 years ago. Sometimes found near the fossils were lances and stone-tipped weapons that could be launched like missiles. But 11,000 years ago is also the same time as the last glacial episode at the end of the Ice Age. For this reason, some scientists favor climate change as the cause of the big mammal extinctions. Of course, both factors may have played a role.

OVERPOPULATION. The problem of too many people on earth. Through the 1990s world population is expected to grow at an average rate of ten thousand more people per hour, almost 88 million a year. Most of this growth will occur in developing countries in the tropics.

Expanding numbers of people make huge demands on the environment. The threat to the tropical rain forest, where there are more plant and animal species than anywhere else on earth, is severe. More people mean more trees are cut down for new homes, farms, and firewood; more wild animals are hunted and wild plants collected; more rivers and lakes are polluted; and more soil is lost.

Recent famines in Africa were not caused by drought. The drought was only the trigger. The cause is the long-term breakdown of the environment. Too many people have used up too many resources too quickly.

The future of the environment, as well as the food supplies for the world, is partly in the hands of family planners. Many countries of tropical Africa and Asia must slow their growth or face a lower standard of living.

In 1987, the world's population surpassed 5 billion. That number is expected to increase to 11 billion by the year 2050. At that time, the world is expected to achieve zero or replacement population growth—no more than two children per family. If that goal can be reached before 2050, many more species may be saved. (2, 11, 17)

OZONE LAYER. The thin, protective layer of the upper atmosphere. It blocks ultraviolet (UV) radiation from the sun. Without the ozone layer, humans would have many more skin cancers. Many crops would fail. Since two out of three plants are sensitive to UV radiation, there could be big changes in the world's ecosystems. A 10 percent increase in UV radiation over the ocean could kill off most of the phytoplankton, or tiny marine plants. No one knows exactly how much ozone would have to be lost to cause such widespread damage. Yet, if the loss is severe enough, much of life could go extinct.

The ozone layer has already suffered some damage. It has been thinned by chlorofluorocarbons (CFCs) and halons—chemicals used in the manufacture of refrigerants, foam insulation, and solvents, among other things. In the mid 1980s, scientists found a seasonal "hole" in the ozone layer over Antarctica. This prompted a world-wide treaty to reduce the use of CFCs by 50 percent by the year 2000. See also **CHLOROFLUOROCARBONS** and **PHYTOPLANKTON**. (2, 11)

P

PASSENGER PIGEON (*Ectopistes migratorius*). An extinct bird that once graced North American skies. It was sixteen inches long with a streamlined body and long wings and numbered in the millions when the first settlers arrived in the United States in the late 1700s. At that time, it may have been the most numerous bird on earth. Farmers and hunters shot hundreds of thousands of the birds year after year for sport and because the birds had a voracious appetite for grain, fruits, nuts, and other cultivated plants. By 1900, passenger pigeons were extinct in the wild. In 1914, the last passenger pigeon, a female named Martha, died at the Cincinnati Zoo. (4, 8, 13)

PCBs (POLYCHLORINATED BIPHENYLS). A group of oily, synthetic, toxic compounds used in refrigeration, in insulation systems, and as lubricants in manufacturing. PCBs were completely banned in 1979 in the United States, yet traces can still be found in the soil, air, ocean, and animal tissues. PCBs do not break down in the environment. Like DDT, PCBs cause reproductive failure in birds and fish as well as mammals. Dolphins, whales, and seals have all been found with high concentrations of PCBs. (11, 13)

PEREGRINE FALCON (*Falco peregrinus*). A bird of prey, once abundant almost worldwide. Between the 1940s, when the pesticide DDT was introduced, and the early 1960s, the peregrine falcon was nearly eliminated from Europe and North America. There were no falcons left in the eastern United States where the heaviest DDT use occurred. DDT picked up in the falcons' food (small birds and ground mammals) made their eggs so thin that they cracked when incubated. The use of DDT in the United States stopped in 1972.

In the early 1970s, a captive breeding program from Cornell University in New York succeeded in breeding and releasing the species into their former range. The chicks returned to hunting wild prey, swooping at speeds of up to 200 miles per hour and grasping it in their talons. Today, with the help of captive breeding, peregrine falcons are returning to North America and Europe. They are even nesting on downtown buildings in large cities. See also **DDT.** (5, 13)

PERIODIC EXTINCTIONS, THEORY OF. The theory that mass extinctions of species have occurred every 26 million years. This view of the fossil record starts with the mass extinction from Late Permian time, about 250 million years ago, and includes the most recent crisis 11 million years ago. It is a much debated theory that has changed as new data comes in on the dates of mass extinctions.

If mass extinctions on earth were periodic, the logical cause is extraterrestrial. An astronomical cause is best able to follow a precise schedule because of the regular rotation of planets and other bodies and the movements of stars. But one problem is that most extinctions seem to be multi-step events spread over hundreds of thousands or millions of years. One scientist suggests the trigger for mass extinctions on earth may be "comet showers." The search continues for causes of extinction—and more proof of their periodic nature. See also **EXTRATERRESTRIAL CAUSES OF EXTINCTION** and **MASS EXTINCTIONS.** (15)

PHYTOPLANKTON. Tiny drifting marine plants that are the basis of life in the ocean. They live only in the sunny top layer of the sea because they need sunlight for photosynthesis. They depend on ocean currents to bring nutrients up near the surface, mostly from the dead bodies of millions of tiny sea animals. Most of this "upwelling" occurs in polar and cold temperate waters—the most productive ocean regions.

Phytoplankton sustains almost all life in the sea. It provides food for zooplankton, tiny marine animals that in turn provide food for fish, squid, and even some whales. If something goes wrong anywhere in this food chain, many animals will die.

Threats to phytoplankton include the greenhouse effect and ozone loss. Global warming from the greenhouse effect could warm the ocean and prevent much of it from upwelling. Without upwelling, phytoplankton would be far less productive. Most life in the sea would die. This would happen over a number of years, perhaps decades. More sudden would be the effect of ozone loss, even if it increased ultraviolet radiation by as little as 10 percent. This could stop photosynthesis and kill off most sea life in a single season. See also **GREENHOUSE EFFECT** and **OZONE LAYER.** (1, 11)

PLEISTOCENE AGE. The epoch or time from 1.8 million to 10,000 years ago. The Pleistocene is often called the "Ice Age," though the Ice Age began a million years earlier in the mid-Pliocene Age. During twenty episodes of glaciation in the Ice Age, many plants and animals went extinct. The most recent extinctions were of large mammals such as the mammoth, mastodon, and sabertooth tiger. These extinctions occurred at the end of the Pleistocene, about 11,000 years ago, and may have been caused by Stone Age hunters. See also **CLIMATE** or **CLIMATIC CHANGE, ICE AGE**, and **OVERKILL HYPOTHESIS.** (14, 15)

POACHING. The illegal killing of animals, mainly for profit, through the wildlife trade. Poachers often work in gangs, armed with high-powered rifles. They work from four-wheel-drive trucks, boats, and even airplanes. In Africa, a poacher after elephant ivory can make more money in an afternoon than a park ranger there makes in a year. Rangers in some parts of Africa will shoot poachers on sight. But the poachers are often more heavily armed.

Poaching poses a major threat to several endangered species such as the giant panda, rhinoceros, cheetah and many other wild cats, and various sea turtles. Poaching for ivory may yet endanger the African elephant whose population was cut in half in the 1980s.

Poaching can also refer to illegal taking of plants. Wild cactus species from the U.S. Southwest and México are prized as house plants and fetch prices of $25 to $1,000 or more. One quarter of the cactus family is now in danger of extinction. See also **GIANT PANDA, IVORY TRADE, OVERHUNTING**, and **WILDLIFE TRADE.** (3, 4, 5, 8, 11, 13)

PREDATOR CONTROL. Programs to kill predators such as wolves and coyotes that sometimes kill farm animals, or seals that feed on fish. Predator control programs have been used in North America since the days of the early settlers. To protect the interests of farmers, ranchers, and fishermen, the U. S. government has in the past offered "bounties" or rewards for killing animals that appear to be "pests." Methods of elimination include leg-hold traps and guns of every sort. Even machine guns and hand grenades were used on seals and sea lions on their remote, rocky colonies off the west coast and Alaska.

Through most of the twentieth century, a wide variety of poisons, such as strychnine, have also been used for predator control. The poisons are left as bait, to help ranchers get rid of wolves, coyotes, and other land predators. By accident, however, eagles and other birds, dogs, and livestock often took the bait. By the 1970s, predator control had caused the extinction of the red wolf in the wild. It has also been a major cause of endangering other wolf species, the grizzly bear, and the swift fox.

Science has shown the value of predators in the natural environment, and most conservationists oppose predator control. Some government wildlife management agencies, however, continue to practice predator control, to limit the numbers of a species. The issue of predator control remains highly controversial. The government must respond to requests from farmers, ranchers, and fishermen. Yet with human populations expanding and encroaching on animal habitats, human needs may overwhelm those of animals, especially large predators. Although predator control is practiced more carefully than in the past, it may yet be a cause for endangering animals and causing others to go extinct. See also **PREDATOR-PREY INTERACTIONS** and **STRYCHNINE.** (13)

PREDATOR-PREY INTERACTIONS. The behavior between predator species and prey species. There is a dynamic balance between predators and prey. Predators need their prey, but prey also need their predators.

When there are more predators than prey, the predators die for lack of food until the prey can produce more offspring. When there are more prey than predators, the predators tend to increase until the prey are then reduced.

Predators keep a prey species healthy by taking mostly the weak, sick, and extra young animals. The agility of prey, on the other hand, keeps predators healthy. Only the faster, stronger, and healthier predators catch the prey. Without prey, predators will die. Without predators, a prey species, too, can be in danger. Prey populations tend to multiply and eat all their available food resources. They then face starvation.

Predator-prey interactions are a feature of every ecosystem. Some ecosystems have many different predators. Some predators may in turn be prey for larger animals. In the tropical rain forest, ants that specialize in eating tiny beetles or other insects are in turn part of a meal for giant anteaters.

Predator-prey interactions help support the diversity of life on earth. The breakdown of these relationships, by killing off a predator such as in predator control programs, disrupts the ecosystem. The big predators are the first to suffer and are the most likely to go extinct. But in the long run, prey too can suffer. See also **PREDATOR CONTROL.** (10, 13)

PREDATORY BEHAVIOR. When an animal hunts, catches, and/or feeds on another animal. Predatory behavior is an indispensable part of the process of how life has evolved on earth. Normally, it does not cause extinction. An exception is when an exotic predator species is introduced to an island or other ecosystem that has never known such predators. See also **EXOTICS** and **PREDATOR-PREY INTERACTIONS.**

PRIMATES. The order of mammals to which humans, apes, monkeys, lemurs, baboons, gibbons, gorillas, and chimpanzees belong. They mainly live in the tropics of Africa, Asia, and South America. Many rare species are found on the islands of Indonesia and Madagascar. About 35 percent of the 190 primate species in the world are endangered. Most of the others are threatened, at least locally. Their decline has mostly come in recent decades with the destruction of the forest for farms, ranches, and wood supplies.

Lemurs, one of the major groups of primates, live only on the island nation of Madagascar. Since humans arrived on Madagascar 1500 years ago, at least thirteen species of lemurs have gone extinct, as more than 90 percent of the island's forests have been cut down. There are now twenty-two species of lemurs left. See also **MADAGASCAR** and **MAMMAL EXTINCTIONS.** (3, 13)

PROTECTED AREA. A natural or mostly natural area set aside for protection, often with legal status. There are many names for protected areas: nature reserve, wildlife preserve, conservation area, national park, state park, wilderness area, natural area, and ecological reserve, among others. Some are different names for the same thing. The exact name often depends upon the country, state, conservation program, or landowner.

Most existing protected areas were set up for wildlife or nature conservation. The idea was to protect a rare mammal or bird, a grove of trees, or a famous landscape. Over the past decade, the driving force for conservation of natural areas, especially for new areas in the tropics, is protecting a sample of each ecosystem.

For example, Costa Rica, a model country for conservation, has protected pieces of dry, lowland, cloud, and other types of tropical forest, as twenty-eight parks and reserves amounting to more than 1.2 million acres—about 10 percent of Costa Rica's total land area. In Tanzania, protected natural areas amount to about 12 percent of the country; in Botswana, as much as 18 percent. The United States and Canada, on the other hand, have only about 5 percent, though Alaska has a substantial 25 percent. The areas conserved in Canada and the United States, however, are generally better protected than in other countries. By 1988, there were more than 3,500 major protected areas established in 125 countries throughout the world, covering some 1.7 million square miles.

Protected areas that conserve sample ecosystems provide a good start for protecting many plant and animal species from extinction. Many species, however, require more and larger protected areas—especially in tropical forests. A type of protected area called a *biosphere reserve* is an effective way to include local people in the process of conservation. Research and conservation measures must also be aimed at the genetic level. See also **BIOSPHERE RESERVE, COSTA**

RICA, GENETIC RESERVE, and **WILDERNESS AREA.** (5, 7, 10, 11, 16)

PUBLIC LANDS. Land owned by the public and managed through government at the national, state, or provincial level. The loudest conservation debates in the United States, Canada, and many countries around the world occur over the plants and animals found on public lands. Most of U.S. public lands are managed by the Forest Service, the Fish and Wildlife Service, the Bureau of Land Management, and the National Park Service. In Canada most of the country is public land, also called crown land, that is administered mainly through the provincial governments. These lands in both countries are then leased for timber, oil, mining, cattle grazing, and other uses. Because they are public lands, people have a right and a responsibility to determine what their elected representatives will do with these lands. See also **LAND USE.**

R

RADIO-TRACKING. Technique for monitoring animals that range over wide areas. The animals are captured briefly and fitted with a tiny transmitter. As the animal moves through its range, the location, breathing rate, and information about other life processes are sent back to a receiving station. The technique has helped scientists study threatened populations of wolves, polar bears, and even whales at sea.

RADIOCARBON DATING. A method of dating fossils up to about 60,000 years old. Scientists can measure the decay of Carbon-14 in the material. In this way dates can be set that approximate when plants and animals went extinct in the recent fossil record. For rocks and fossils older than 60,000 years, other methods are used.

RECORD. See **FOSSIL RECORD.**

RED DATA BOOKS. Lists of threatened plant and animal species and protected areas around the world. Sponsored by conservation groups, these status reports are being prepared country by country. Red Data Books provide detailed background information needed to conserve threatened species and habitats. They have also helped to publicize conservation needs.

REFORESTATION. Replanting trees to create a new forest. The rate at which new forests have been replanted and regrown has been slower than the rate of cutting. In the temperate forests of the United States, Canada, Europe, and the Soviet Union, replanting has improved in recent years due to increased effort and better techniques. In tropical forests, however, the poor soil in many regions makes replanting difficult. Only one tree is replanted for every ten removed.

Reforestation solves some economic problems, by putting people to work replanting trees. New trees help protect the soil and watersheds, and help slow down the greenhouse effect. But a managed forest cannot replace the original forest in terms of species diversity. There are many more species in the original forest than in managed tree farms designed for maximum wood production.

After a forest burns or is cut down, the plant and animal community changes. A few species may be able to move to the remaining original or mature forest, but most species will suffer losses and some may even go extinct. Some of the area cut will return in natural regeneration, although it may take centuries to replace what once grew. Many forests today are cut on a rotation basis, but within a few decades throughout the world, all of the commercial original growth forest not set aside in protected areas will be gone.

To keep the diverse ecosystems of tropical and temperate forests, some large pieces of the primitive forest must be left intact. A diversity of tree species must be allowed to grow without the use of herbicides or other chemicals. One type of reforestation that aims to replace the entire ecosystem is restoration ecology. See also **CLIMAX** or **CLIMAX COMMUNITY** and **RESTORATION ECOLOGY.** (2, 5, 7, 11, 12, 17)

REFUGIUM (plural: **REFUGIA**). A place that escaped the effects of climate change. During the last episode of the Ice Age, for example, glaciers spreading over North America left certain high areas ice-free.

Such areas became refuges for various plants and animals called relic species. These species—often in whole relic communities—reveal the ways of an earlier era. It is important to preserve refugia from any human development. Refugia yet hold some of the survivors of the extinctions of the past and are fascinating areas to study evolution. See also **RELIC SPECIES.**

REHABILITATION. See **RESTORATION ECOLOGY.**

REINTRODUCTION OF SPECIES. To return a species to its natural habitat. Reintroducing species is the goal of most captive breeding programs of threatened or endangered animals and plants. For many programs, however, it is a long-term goal, one hard to attain.

To succeed, a reintroduction program should try to return individual plants or animals from as diverse a population as available yet genetically similar to those that were there before. Captive birds and mammals in particular must also shake their dependence on human caretakers for food, shelter, and protection. Half-way houses or enclosures, plus monitoring after release, help to ease the species' adjustment period.

There have been a few successes. The Hawaiian goose has been returned from England to Hawaii. The Arabian oryx, once extinct in the wild, has now been returned to the desert region of Oman. And pilot whales, stranded on a Cape Cod beach and near death, were rescued by an aquarium and returned to the wild six months later. Aquarium staff fixed radio-tags to monitor the movements of the three whales. The whales found a group of pilot whales in the open sea and joined it. (5, 13)

RELIC SPECIES. Plants or animals surviving from an earlier time. Many relic species are endangered, found only on an island or a refugium left over from the last Ice Age episode. See also **ENDEMIC SPECIES** and **REFUGIUM.**

REPRODUCTION. The process by which plants or animals give rise to offspring. Plants and animals reproduce in a variety of ways. Most animals reproduce sexually, combining sperm from the male and an egg from the female. This method allows for greater genetic diversity in offspring. Many plants use two methods: They reproduce sexually through pollination to give their progeny genetic diversity. But at times they also reproduce by cloning to increase their numbers.

The manner or timing of reproduction can affect a plant's or animal's chances of survival as a species. Animals particularly in danger of extinction are those that reproduce late in life, such as elephants (age thirty or more) and certain whale species (age fourteen or more), and have a low birth rate (one baby per mother every two to three years or more). Plants that flower for limited times or have only one pollinator can also be in danger. The reproduction of a plant or animal must be considered in any management program. See also **COEVOLVED RELATIONSHIP.**

REPRODUCTIVE ISOLATION. When members of similar species do not reproduce even though they may be geographically close. Species remain distinct because their members cannot interbreed with members of other species.

REPTILE EXTINCTIONS. The end of certain species of reptiles. As a group, reptiles evolved about 300 million years ago. They rose to great prominence during the Mesozoic Era, which began 248 million years ago. Many of them went extinct at the end of the Cretaceous period, 65 million years ago. The cause is thought to be climate change from meteorites or comets hitting the earth or perhaps from the explosion of a volcano. The few reptiles that survive today are here because their ancestors survived that mass extinction. Some of them, such as sea turtles, look very much as they did back then. Other modern reptiles include many species of lizards, snakes, alligators, and crocodiles.

At least twenty species of reptiles have gone extinct since the year 1600. Most are due to the introduction of exotic species on islands. Six species of lizards and snakes went extinct on islands of the West Indies from introduced mongooses and cats.

The threats to reptiles today come primarily from commercial hunters and habitat destruction. Sea turtles, for example, have been killed for their meat, oil, eggs, leather, and tortoise shell. Crocodiles and alligators are used for shoes and luggage. The zoo and pet trades also account for some threats to reptiles.

Almost a hundred species of reptiles are threatened or endangered and are listed on the U.S. Endangered Species List. See also **CLIMATE** or **CLIMATIC CHANGE, EXTRATERRESTRIAL CAUSES OF EXTINCTION**, and **SEA TURTLES.** (4, 5, 11, 13, 14, 15)

RESTORATION ECOLOGY. The science of restoring degraded land to its original wild condition. Restoration ecology is a fairly new idea but interest in it is growing around the world, especially in the tropics. With more than half of all tropical rain forests cut down, and more destroyed every year, restoration ecology is needed to provide homes for endangered species. But it is very time-consuming, costly work.

To build a new forest, for example, ecologists try to mimic the stages of the forest. They start with the plant and animal communities that recolonize the land after fire or disaster and move step-by-step to the climax forest that grows many years later. Their techniques include: (1) cataloging everything in existing forests at various stages, to learn about all the parts of the forest; (2) using forest animals such as birds to do the work of spreading seeds; (3) helping new forests get started around a central colonizing tree; (4) providing a variety of ecosystems from high to low and dry to wet to provide refuges for animals as the weather changes from day to day; and (5) teaching local people to appreciate snakes and other animals, to use the plants wisely, and to enjoy and protect the forest.

Using these and other ideas, American scientist Daniel Janzen is trying to rebuild a tropical rain forest along the Pacific coast of northwestern Costa Rica. He is converting mainly abandoned lands into part of a park or protected area. To get local people involved, he is making outside areas of the park available for recreation, farming, and other uses. Janzen is trying to conserve biological diversity in a way that is consistent with human values. See also **BIOSPHERE RESERVE, CLIMAX** or **CLIMAX COMMUNITY** and **REFOREST-ATION.**

ROSY PERIWINKLE. A small plant with purple flowers native to the drier tropical forests of Madagascar. Two powerful drugs are made from biocompounds found a few years ago in the leaves of the rosy periwinkle. These drugs now cure most cases of Hodgkin's disease and childhood leukemia. The rosy periwinkle was an overlooked plant in the forests of Madagascar, 90 percent of which have been cut down. Now the rosy periwinkle is cultivated in many countries and protected in some cases in the wild. See also **MADAGASCAR.** (11, 12)

S

SANCTUARY. See **PROTECTED AREA.**

SEA TURTLES. Turtles of a number of species that live in the sea, mainly in the tropics and warm temperate zones. Sea turtles crawl out on beaches to lay their eggs in the sand. Among those threatened or endangered are the loggerhead, Kemp's ridley, green, hawksbill, and leatherback, all of which are seen in North American waters.

The steep decline, in most cases, has only come in recent decades. Turtles such as the loggerhead, which is found around the world, are caught for food and curios. They lose their nesting sites to resorts and houses along the beach. Their main cause of death, however, is drowning in shrimp nets. In U.S. waters alone, shrimp fishermen accidentally catch and kill over 11,000 sea turtles a year, most of them loggerheads.

U.S. government researchers have devised special fishing gear called the TED that deflects the turtles away from the net. U.S. shrimpers, though, have been slow to adopt the device. It costs about $200 per net and there is some effort required to modify their nets. But shrimpers in other countries such as Indonesia use the TED as required by law and kill few sea turtles. See also **TED.** (5, 13)

SEED BANKS. A method of conserving plant genes, in which seeds are dried and stored below freezing. Seed banks are the most common and convenient form of genebank conservation.

Most seeds are small. Hundreds may fit in a packet or jar. Each seed of a species has a different genetic constitution. Thus a wide range of genes may be included in one sample in a small container.

Most countries of the world now have seed banks. These national seedbanks are set up mainly to conserve crop species and their wild relatives. Many species can be stored for decades, up to 100 years. But seeds must be grown out eventually before they go bad and be replaced with newly harvested seeds.

For wild species, seed banks can help prevent extinction and they make the species available to plant breeders and scientists. But wild species, taken into a seed bank, can no longer benefit from natural processes in the wild. They cannot usually be pollinated by insects. They stop evolving. The best way to conserve the genes of wild plants is through protected areas where the wild species can continue to evolve defenses against diseases and insect pests. See **EX SITU GENETIC CONSERVATION** and **GENEBANK.** (5, 11, 12)

SKIN TRADE. See **WILDLIFE TRADE.**

SLASH AND BURN AGRICULTURE. The practice of cutting and burning all the vegetation on a piece of land, planting crops, then moving to another plot of land to repeat the process as the original land declines. Also called *swidden agriculture,* slash and burn is common in tropical forests where most soils are poor. Cutting and burning the trees releases the nutrients held in the vegetation. These nutrients then fertilize the soil. For one to three years, crops thrive until the excess nutrients are gone. Then the farmer moves on, repeating the process, while the land recovers. In some tropical forests, such as the Amazon, the land must be allowed to lie fallow for at least fourteen years. Where the areas cleared are large and the soil continues to be disturbed by cattle grazing, the land may take many more years to recover.

Slash and burn agriculture can work on a small scale if farmers rotate the plots of land they cultivate. However, millions of people moving into Brazil's Amazon and other tropical forests are practicing this method. In the process, tropical forests and delicate tropical soils are being destroyed. (7, 12, 16)

SOIL EROSION. The loss of soil, mainly the topsoil that has the nutrients to support plant growth. Worldwide, about 32 million acres of good farm land are lost each year due to erosion.

Soil, a precious resource, comes from hundreds of years of living things growing, dying, and decomposing. Once cleared, if the land is left unprotected, the soil is exposed to the full force of the sun, rain, and wind. It can be blown or washed away in a season. Farmlands left bare for part of each year suffer some of the worst soil erosion.

Soil erosion often occurs after deforestation and can lead to desertification. Soil erosion does not directly cause animals or plants to go extinct, but it is part of a destructive process in which land loses its ability to sustain life. When a country loses large areas to soil erosion, more pressure is placed on governments to convert wild lands and protected areas with rare or endangered species into farmland. See also **DEFORESTATION** and **DESERTIFICATION.** (11, 12, 17)

SPECIES INTRODUCTIONS. See **EXOTICS.**

SPOTTED OWL, NORTHERN *(Strix occidentalis caurina).* A rare owl species found in the northwest United States. This species lives only in large areas of old growth or primitive forest, mostly on federal land managed by the U.S. Forest Service. It depends on standing dead trees, or snags, for its habitat. After the past century of cutting in the northwest, an estimated 10 to 30 percent of old growth forest remains.

In 1988, U.S. Fish and Wildlife Service biologists determined that the northern spotted owl should be put on the endangered species list which would give it full federal protection. Timber companies that cut old growth in national forests lobbied in Congress, saying that protecting the spotted owl would mean the loss of one third of their timber harvest and many jobs in the region. In 1990, the northern spotted owl was named a threatened species, entitling the bird, and thousands of acres of habitat, to protection. The timber companies are fighting the decision.

STELLER'S SEA COW *(Hydrodamalis gigas)*. An extinct species in an order of plant-eating marine mammals. This giant species—up to twenty-six feet long and seven tons—was discovered off Alaska when the scientist George W. Steller was shipwrecked on Bering Island in 1741. Steller found them tame and liked to watch them eat and play in the shallows. They swam in groups of ten to twenty. At that time there were perhaps only a few thousand sea cows, all living on a few islands in the North Pacific. They were used as food by Steller and later expeditions to the area. They soon became victims of overhunting. In 1768, twenty-seven years after their discovery, Russian sailors ate the last Steller's sea cow. (4)

STRYCHNINE. A poison used to kill animals, mainly predators such as wolves. Strychnine has been a part of predator control programs in North America since the 1930s. Many programs in the United States and Canada have been government-sponsored. Farmers and ranchers have used strychnine and other poisons to protect their lands and livestock from wolves, foxes, coyotes, and bears. The poison, left as bait, was highly effective in eliminating many animals; in fact, it helped drive some wolf and fox species to extinction. It has also killed not only predators but eagles, ferrets, dogs, and sometimes even livestock—any animal that happens to eat it. Ravens and many other birds that feed on poisoned dead animals have also been killed. When the poison has seeped into water systems, it has killed humans, too.

In 1972, because of their deadly effectiveness on rare and endangered species, strychnine and other poisons were banned for use on federal land. Yet ranchers and others continued to pressure Congress, claiming that they needed poison to protect their livestock. In 1982, strychnine was reapproved for more controlled use on a limited basis. Many biologists and conservationists, however, disagree with bringing it back. See also **PREDATOR CONTROL.** (13)

SUSTAINABLE DEVELOPMENT. The wise use of the earth's resources, according to the principles of conservation. The survival of humans depends on a continuous supply of many resources, including water, trees, soil, air, and minerals. Sustainable development of the ocean, for example, means catching fish at a rate that can be sustained indefinitely. This approach ensures that fishermen will be able to keep their livelihood and that fish will not become endangered or go extinct. The concept of sustainable development could be useful for managing most of the earth's resources. In practice, however, it is difficult to limit industrial development. Unless carefully regulated, fishermen (or other resource users) tend to take as much as they can until there is nothing left.

Sustainable development is the key phrase of the World Conservation Strategy as well as the World Commission on Environment and Development—two attempts to bring the idea of conservation into the arena of world planning and decision-making. See also **CONSERVATION** and **WORLD CONSERVATION STRATEGY.** (5, 11)

T

TAXONOMY or **SYSTEMATICS.** The science of classifying living things into species, families, orders, and kingdoms. The names are in Latin and are in use around the world, a practice which aids the exchange of information among scientists and wildlife managers from different countries. To scientists, the name of a plant or animal is the key to all that is written about it and all future research.

Taxonomy, however, is much more than giving names to species. It requires a study of a species' habits, its basic biology, and its evolutionary history. Much conservation and scientific work depends on good taxonomy. Without knowing the basic facts and needs of a plant or animal, there can be no conservation. Yet in the tropical rain forest, most species, particularly insects, have yet to be named or even seen. To date, 1.7 million species have been named on earth, but most of the work has been done on species in the north temperate zone. Scientists estimate there are at least 4.4 million species but recent work in the tropical rain forest may push world totals to more than 30 million species. Many may go extinct in the next few decades before they are ever discovered or given a name by taxonomists. There is a widely recognized need for more scientists and more funding to work on tropical taxonomy. Such work could help save many more species from extinction. See also **BIOLOGICAL DIVERSITY.** (1, 2, 10, 16)

TED (TURTLE EXCLUDER DEVICE or **TRAWLING EFFI-
CIENCY DEVICE).** A metal cagelike device sewn into a trawl net
used by shrimp fishermen. It allows turtles to escape while the shrimp
remain. The main purpose of the TED, developed by the U.S. government and first tested in 1981, is to save sea turtles from drowning in
nets. See also **SEA TURTLES.**

THREATENED SPECIES. A plant or animal species likely to
become endangered in the near future in all or a main portion of its
natural habitat. "Threatened" is also a legal status under the U.S.
Endangered Species Act. The protection for threatened species ranges
from a simple listing of the species, so that there is a recognition of its
status, to full protection similar to that given to an endangered species.
See also **ENDANGERED SPECIES LIST.**

TISSUE CULTURE. A method of conserving genes in which little
plants or plant tissues are grown slowly in tubes of nutrients. Plant
tissue culture is also called the *in vitro* method, which means "in
glass."

Tissue culture has been used in genebanks to slow down the
growth and conserve for a time certain crop varieties and their wild
relatives, such as potatoes, cassava, sweet potatoes, and pears. Tissue
culture research focuses on species that do not form seeds well or
whose seeds cannot be dried and cooled without injury. But tissue
culture research takes time and money. Much research needs to be
done to judge the long-term genetic effects and to find the right
techniques for each species. The future may lie in cryopreservation—
the long-term storage of frozen tissue cultures at low temperatures
(down to -196° C.). See also *EX SITU* **GENETIC CONSERVA-
TION, GENEBANK,** and **SEED BANK.** (5, 11)

TOURISM. The travel industry. Tourism can be a powerful force for conserving protected areas, but it can also contribute to the extinction of species. Adventure travel is a large and fast-growing segment of tourism, the world's largest industry. Adventure travel includes hiking, skiing, canoeing, kayaking, trail riding, river rafting, scuba diving, nature observation, and photography.

On the plus side, these activities help to provide an economic return for protected areas. In the world today, pristine lands are in demand for logging, farms, ranches, and other uses. In general, keeping the land wild is a long-term investment—both in terms of conserving biological diversity and for tourism. In the African nations of Kenya and Tanzania, which have set aside large wildlife reserves, visitors from around the world come to see lions, giraffes, gazelles, and many other large mammals. With trained guides, the impact on the land and the animals is small, and the money from tourists helps to employ local people.

Costa Rica also has a system of national parks and reserves, some of which cater to visiting scientists and nature lovers eager to see the tropical rain forest. Visitors stay in cabins at the edge of the jungle and guides show them everything from rain forest army ants to spider and howler monkeys screeching in the treetops. When these visitors return home, they are often keen to conserve the world's rain forest.

Some endangered species or habitats may be too sensitive to withstand much tourism. Dune grasses along beaches and in deserts hold down the soil and help maintain the desert ecosystem. But these plants can be easily destroyed by too many hikers or even a few week-end motorcycles and other off-road-vehicles. Sea-side developments—hotels and beach houses—have ruined some areas. Yet most places can contend with some visitor traffic. If these places can be kept wild, yet give tourists the message about conservation and earn some money, tourism will be playing an important part in conservation. See also **CONSERVATION.** (5)

TROPICAL CANOPIES. See **CANOPY (OF THE TROPICAL RAIN FOREST).**

TROPICAL RAIN FOREST. An evergreen forest with more than a hundred inches of rain a year and fairly constant, warm temperatures. Tropical rain forests are found in a wide band around the equator, mostly in South and Central America, central Africa, and southeast Asia and nearby islands.

These forests are the most productive biome on earth. They are the home of more than half of the world's plant and animal species. At present, the area of tropical rain forest remaining in the world is about 2.3 million square miles, about three-quarters the size of the continental United States. This area is about half of the original total. Every year some 80,000 square miles are cut or damaged, an area the size of Kansas. The land is being cleared for farms and cattle ranches and cut by the logging industry.

In tropical rain forests, an estimated 1,000 species of plants and animals are going extinct each year. Scientists predict the extinction rate will increase. Over the next thirty years, if the current rate of cutting continues, an estimated 1.1 million species, at least one quarter of the biological diversity on earth, will likely go extinct. See also **BIOLOGICAL DIVERSITY, CANOPY (OF THE TROPICAL RAIN FOREST)**, and **DEFORESTATION.** (1, 2, 5, 7, 11, 12, 16, 17)

TRUMPETER SWAN. Largest of all waterfowl with a wingspread of eight feet. The species mates for life and fiercely protects its family. Native to the western United States and Canada, they declined quickly and drew close to extinction in the second half of the nineteenth century due to the wildlife trade. Their feathers were taken for ladies' hats and writing quills. Their down was used to make powder puffs.

In the 1920s, Ralph Edwards began feeding a flock of about thirty-five swans wintering at Lonesome Lake, British Columbia. He loved the swans and took care of them year after year, only learning later that his visitors were among the last of their kind. In response to such wildlife management efforts and the end of hunting these birds, they have begun to recover. From a low of perhaps 100 swans at the turn of the century, they have increased in number today to more than 10,000, mainly in Alaska. See also **WILDLIFE TRADE.** (13)

TUNA-PORPOISE FISHERY. Fishing in the eastern tropical Pacific Ocean in which fishermen follow and set their nets around dolphins (or porpoises, as the fishermen call them) in order to catch tuna fish. As the fishermen close the nets and pull in their catch, many dolphins get tangled in the net and drown. The number killed has declined in recent years, but it still amounts to about 100,000 dolphins a year. Several species of dolphins are taken. None of these species is considered endangered, but at least one is thought to be rare. Conservationists have called for stricter controls and for more care to be taken during the netting to limit the number killed. They have also said that people should stop eating tuna to send a message to the fishermen. In 1990, most U.S. tuna companies responded by refusing to buy tuna caught around dolphins. Most dolphins, however, are killed by foreign tuna fishermen. But because the U.S. eats 40 percent of the world's tuna, many foreign fishermen may soon be forced to stop killing dolphins, too. (9)

V–Z

VOLCANIC SCENARIO. The idea that mass extinctions might have been caused by climate change after the eruption of volcanoes. A thin layer of clay with the element iridium has been found in the fossil record at sites all over the world. Many scientists believe iridium comes from meteorites hitting the earth, but it might also have come from volcanoes.

In the volcanic scenario, one or more eruptions might have put enough dust in the air to block the sun and stop photosynthesis. Plants would have withered and died, and many animals would have starved. See also **EXTRATERRESTRIAL CAUSES OF EXTINCTION.** (14, 15)

WETLANDS AND AQUATIC ECOSYSTEMS. Ecosystems where land and water meet, including freshwater marshes, estuaries or salt marshes, and mangroves. Wetlands act as natural reservoirs that help to regulate the flow of rivers. They prevent floods by absorbing excess water in wet seasons and slowly releasing it during the year. They can even help purify polluted water.

Wetlands are rich in plant and animal species. The land beneath the water nourishes the plants or trees, which in turn enrich the ecosystem. Some fish use these areas to breed and find sanctuary. Migratory birds use them as summering or wintering grounds or stop-offs.

Estuaries, washed by both fresh water and salt water, are the richest wetlands. They serve as nurseries for shrimp, crabs, and about two thirds of all commercial salt water fishes. Wetlands are so numerous and diverse that there are no reliable worldwide estimates for their original and present extent. Over the past two centuries, however, an estimated half of the wetlands in the United States have been destroyed. See also **MANGROVES** and **WETLANDS DESTRUCTION.**

WETLANDS DESTRUCTION. The destruction of freshwater marshes, estuaries, and mangroves. For centuries in Europe and North America, marshes have been treated as wasteland—used for dumping rubbish and sewage—or filled in as farmland. Coastal wetlands in estuaries have been "reclaimed" as cities were built. Since estuaries are at the mouths of rivers, they are prime sites for ports. About half of all wetlands in the United States have been destroyed.

Some thirty-one bird species—such as the Hermit Ibis and the Dalmatian Pelican—have been endangered by the draining of marshes.

Along the coasts of India and Sri Lanka, mangroves are being cut for firewood, making things difficult for local fishermen. The cutting destroys the shrimp and crab habitat, as well as the breeding grounds for fish.

In 1971, an international agreement was drafted to identify and protect wetlands. The Convention on Wetlands of International Importance (RAMSAR) has listed 329 wetlands covering 75,000 square miles. To date, 34 countries are participating in RAMSAR, but many more must sign on if the agreement is to conserve a network of the world's wetlands. (5, 11, 13, 17)

WHALING. See **WILDLIFE TRADE.**

WILD RELATIVES OF CROPS. Wild species and varieties of plants related to crops and other economic plants. These wild species are used to breed crops that can resist pests and disease. The modern tomato could not exist as we know it without genes from its nine wild relatives from the west coast of South America. Besides pest and disease resistance, the tomato's wild relatives offer increased vitamin content, better fruit color, and resistance to drought and salt water. Some of the grape and the soybeans's wild relatives have helped adapt these crops to the colder areas of the Soviet Union.

The conservation of wild relatives is crucial to the world's future food supply. Wild relatives have the potential to help crops adapt to the drier, hotter weather that may result from global warming from the greenhouse effect. They may also help Africa develop more productive, drought-resistant crops.

Wild relatives need to be conserved in both genebanks and in the wild. A start has been made on their conservation in seed banks, but much remains to be done. The task of conserving them in the wild is expensive and time-consuming. See also **ECONOMIC BOTANY** and *IN SITU* **GENETIC CONSERVATION.** (5, 12)

WILDERNESS AREA. A kind of protected area without roads and set aside from all industrial use. Wilderness areas form part of the U.S. system of public lands. Since the Wilderness Act was passed in 1964, more than 90 million acres have become part of the National Wilderness Preservation System. These lands may function as genetic reserves for some rare and endangered species of plants and animals. See also **BIOSPHERE RESERVE** and **PROTECTED AREA.** (26)

WILDLIFE MANAGEMENT. The management of animal populations in the natural habitat. Today, a solid wildlife management program starts with the duties of an ecologist working in nature. It includes research into abundance, population, reproductive biology, ecology, and social behavior. It may involve research in captivity on captive breeding and reintroduction, animal stress, and diseases. Wildlife management must also consider the human impact on wildlife. Sometimes programs are needed to change the attitudes of poachers, developers, safari hunters, farmers, and ranchers.

Major gaps in our knowledge about rare and endangered species remain. Some biologists feel there may be only a few years left to study the natural populations of many species. In the past, good wildlife management meant "simply leaving a species alone." But studies are crucial now. Most wildlife managers agree that soon all species will need active management. See also **CONSERVATION** and **PROTECTED AREA.** (5, 6, 10, 11, 13, 18, 19, 20, 21, 22, 23, 24, 25)

WILDLIFE PRESERVE. See **PROTECTED AREA.**

WILDLIFE SMUGGLING. See **WILDLIFE TRADE.**

WILDLIFE TRADE. Legal and illegal trade in live animals and their products. After habitat destruction, wildlife trade is the most common cause driving animals toward extinction.

Animals endangered by the wildlife trade include many species of wild cats for their fur, birds for their feathers, and reptiles for their skins. Other animals are wanted for zoo animals and exotic pets.

Through human history, the wildlife trade's biggest prizes have been the whales. Oil from the blubber of whales lit the lamps of early America. The different parts of whales were also used to make soap, lipstick, corset stays, umbrella ribs, and meat. About fifteen species of whales have been hunted since commercial whaling began in earnest two centuries ago. Although whaling has mostly stopped, species such as northern right whales may yet go extinct because only about 500 animals are left.

The history of the fur trade shows that few animals, no matter how abundant, can avoid near extinction if their skin is valuable. In North America alone, the bison, sea otter, marten, fisher, and kit fox were once common. The American, European, and Japanese markets have also sponsored the near extinction of fur seals, chinchillas, spotted cats such as jaguars, various leopards, cheetahs, and ocelots.

In recent decades there have been attempts to stem the wildlife trade for endangered animals. Many countries have passed laws protecting certain animals or forbidding the import or export of their products. But regional and sometimes world-wide agreements are needed because the wildlife trade goes between countries. The International Whaling Commission (IWC) was set up in 1946 to manage the whales. Only in the 1980s, however, has it helped to stop the killing of whales.

A big step toward control of the wildlife trade was a treaty drafted in 1973 called "CITES"—the Convention on International Trade in Endangered Species. CITES prohibits commercial trade around the world in the rarest 600 or so species of animals and plants. To date, more than 100 countries have signed the CITES treaty. Yet some countries such as Japan, using loopholes in the agreement, still import huge quantities of tortoise shell, crocodile skins, and other wildlife products.

Some conservation groups, frustrated with the slow progress, have taken matters into their own hands. Greenpeace, for example, has fought the wildlife trade by going to sea in small boats and blocking the killing of whales in the North Pacific and the Antarctic. They brought along TV camera operators to film the deaths of the whales. These images, shown to millions of people, helped to build popular support for the whales and to hasten the end of almost all whaling.

But the main way to stop wildlife trade is to cut the demand. With the wildlife trade worth billions of dollars a year, it is hard to stop. In 1989, CITES countries voted for a ban on all ivory imports to protect the African elephant. Smuggling will continue, but it will be more difficult to sell the ivory. See also **IVORY TRADE and OVER-HUNTING.** (4, 5, 9, 11, 13, 20, 22, 25)

WORLD CONSERVATION STRATEGY. A plan launched in 1980 by conservation groups and the United Nations to help the countries of the world deal with global environmental problems. The plan has three main points: (1) Plant and animal populations must be kept healthy. (2) The basic life-support systems of earth—climate, soils, water, air—must be conserved if life is to continue. (3) Biological diversity is the key to the future. These conservation goals were promoted through the idea of "sustainable development." Since 1980, many countries have set up national conservation strategies based on these principles. See also **BIOLOGICAL DIVERSITY** and **SUSTAINABLE DEVELOPMENT.** (5, 11, 17)

ZOOS. See **CAPTIVE BREEDING.**

FOR FURTHER INFORMATION

GOVERNMENT AGENCIES

Forest Service
Department of Agriculture
P.O. Box 96090
Washington, DC 20090
(202) 447-4211

National Marine Fisheries Service
1335 East/West Highway
Silver Spring, MD 20910
(301) 443-8910

National Park Service
Department of the Interior
Room 3043
Washington, DC 20240
(202) 343-7394

Fish & Wildlife Service
Department of the Interior
18th and C Streets, NW
Mail Stop 725
Arlington Square Building
Washington, DC 20240
ATTENTION: Publications Unit
(202) 358-1711

CONSERVATION AND
ENVIRONMENTAL ORGANIZATIONS

American Cetacean Society
P.O. Box 2639
San Pedro, CA 90731
(213) 548-6279

Animal Welfare Institute
P.O. Box 3650
Washington, DC 20007
(202) 337-2333

**Center for Marine
Conservation**
1725 Desales Street, NW
Suite 500
Washington, DC 20036
(202) 429-5609

Defenders of Wildlife
1244 Nineteenth Street, NW
Washington, DC 20036
(202) 659-9510

Greenpeace U.S.A.
1436 U Street, NW
Washington, DC 20009
(202) 462-1177

National Audubon Society
950 Third Avenue
New York, NY 10022
(212) 832-3200

National Wildlife Federation
1400 16th Street, NW
Washington, DC 20036
(202) 797-6800

The Nature Conservancy
1815 N. Lynn Street
Arlington, VA 22209
(703) 841-5300

Sierra Club
730 Polk Street
San Francisco, CA 94109
(415) 776-2211

World Resources Institute
1709 New York Avenue, NW
Washington, DC 20006
(202) 638-6300

**World Wildlife Fund–
United States**
1250 24th Street, NW
Washington, DC 20037
(202) 293-4800

An annual directory of conservation groups and government agencies is the *Conservation Directory* (**National Wildlife Federation**, 1400 16th Street, NW, Washington, DC 20036).

REFERENCES

BOOKS

1. Blackmore, Stephen and Elizabeth Tootill, eds. *The Penguin Dictionary of Botany*. London: Penguin Books Ltd., 1984.
2. Brown, Lester R., et al., eds. *State of the World 1990*. New York: W. W. Norton and Company, 1990. [Annual]
3. Burton, John A. *The Collins Guide to the Rare Mammals of the World*. Lexington, Mass.: The Stephen Green Press, 1988.
4. Day, David. *The Doomsday Book of Animals*. New York: The Viking Press, 1981.
5. Durrell, Lee. *State of the Ark*. New York: Doubleday, 1986.
6. Forsyth, Adrian. *Mammals of the American North*. Camden East, Ont.: Camden House/Firefly, 1985.
7. Forsyth, Adrian and Ken Miyata. *Tropical Nature*. New York: Charles Scribner's Sons, 1984.
8. Fuller, Errol. *Extinct Birds*. New York: Facts on File Publications, 1987.
9. Hoyt, Erich. *The Whale Watcher's Handbook*. New York: Doubleday, 1984.
10. McFarland, David, ed. *The Oxford Companion to Animal Behavior*. Oxford: Oxford University Press, 1987.
11. Myers, Norman, ed. *Gaia: An Atlas of Planet Management*. New York: Anchor Press/Doubleday & Co. Inc., 1984.
12. Myers, Norman. *The Primary Source*. New York: W. W. Norton & Company, 1984.

13. Nilsson, Greta. *The Endangered Species Handbook.* Washington, D.C.: Animal Welfare Institute, 1986.

14. Simpson, George G. *Fossils and the History of Life.* New York: W. H. Freeman and Company, 1983.

15. Stanley, Steven M. *Extinction.* New York: Scientific American Books, Inc., 1987.

16. Wilson, Edward O. *Biophilia.* Cambridge, Mass.: Harvard University Press, 1984.

17. World Resources Institute, United National Environment Program and the United Nations Development Program. *World Resources 1990–91.* New York: Oxford University Press, 1990. [Biennial]

MAGAZINES

To follow news of endangered plants and animals, try the following magazines available at the library or by subscription:

18. *Audubon*

19. *BioScience*

20. *Defenders*

21. *Equinox*

22. *International Wildlife*

23. *National Geographic*

24. *National Wildlife*

25. *New Scientist*

26. *Wilderness*

27. *World Watch*

28. *Animals Agenda*

ABOUT THE AUTHOR

Erich Hoyt is a writer on science, nature and the environment. He has written seven books based on his experiences with whales and other wildlife from the Arctic to the tropical rain forests. His articles have appeared in more than 100 magazines and newspapers including *National Geographic*, *International Wildlife*, *Defenders*, *The New York Times*, and *The Guardian*.

Mr. Hoyt has worked for the World Wildlife Fund and the International Board for Plant Genetic Resources in Rome. Also, he has lectured at the Massachusetts Institute of Technology, and helped design science exhibits in the United States. He currently lives in Edinburgh, Scotland, with his wife, Sarah Wedden, an embryologist and lecturer, and their son, Mose.